KT-166-987

Macmillan Professional Masters

Marketing for the Non-profit Sector

Macmillan Professional Masters

Titles in the series

Marketing for the Non-profit Sector

Tim Hannagan

MACMILLAN

© Tim Hannagan 1992

All rights reserved. No reproduction, copy or transmission of
this publication may be made without written permission.

No paragraph of this publication may be reproduced, copied or
transmitted save with written permission or in accordance with
the provisions of the Copyright, Designs and Patents Act 1988,
or under the terms of any licence permitting limited copying
issued by the Copyright Licensing Agency, 90 Tottenham Court
Road, London W1P 9HE.

Any person who does any unauthorised act in relation to this
publication may be liable to criminal prosecution and civil
claims for damages.

First published 1992 by
THE MACMILLAN PRESS LTD
Houndmills, Basingstoke, Hampshire RG21 2XS
and London
Companies and representatives
throughout the world

ISBN 0–333–52582–5

A catalogue record for this book is available
from the British Library.

Printed in Great Britain by
Mackays of Chatham PLC
Chatham, Kent

10 9 8 7 6 5 4 3 2
01 00 99 98 97 96 95 94

To Hamish

Contents

Preface

The aim of this book is to provide a comprehensive analysis of marketing in the non-profit sector. The book is designed to cover the fundamental aspects of marketing, and to elucidate the differences between marketing in non-profit organisations and marketing in the profit-making sector of the economy.

The book stresses the importance of marketing for all organisations and its relevance to all institutions in the non-profit sector, including central and local government services, educational institutions, nationalised industries, charities and arts associations. The services that are covered include education, health, social services, leisure and sports facilities, the police force, the armed forces and other non-profit areas such as charities and voluntary societies.

The book is designed to be of use to managers, students and the general reader. The importance of marketing in most non-profit institutions has greatly increased in recent years and general managers, as well as marketing managers, need to have a clear idea of marketing concepts and techniques. At the same time, the majority of people who work in organisations that provide services, whether or not they are managers, need to understand marketing because it is part of their job. As training and development expand in meeting customers', clients' and consumers' needs, marketing will be an increasingly important element of many people's work.

Students on a range of business and management courses, or those studying in areas that include aspects of business and administration, will find that the book fills a major gap in its analysis of the non-profit sector, as well as providing a useful introduction to marketing in general, because it includes all the concepts and techniques of marketing and their applications.

Readers should be able to apply a variety of ideas and methods to help to solve problems in creating a good image for their organisations, in developing excellent lines of communication both within the institution and with consumers and clients, and in promoting a high quality customer-orientated service in order to achieve a clear direction for the activities of the organisation.

TIM HANNAGAN

Acknowledgements

The author and publishers wish to thank the following for permission to use copyright material in the text of this book: BBC Enterprises Limited for extracts reproduced from *Troubleshooter* by John Harvey-Jones with Anthea Massey; Butterworth Heinemann for extracts from *Managing the Non-Profit Organisation* by Peter F. Drucker; Frazer–Nash Consultancy Ltd for extracts from their mission statement; the Local Government Management Board for the use of extracts from its publication *Getting Closer to the Public*; London Borough of Hillingdon for extracts from *The Council's Vision*; Longman Group UK for extracts from *Education*. Metropolitan Police for extracts from the *Plus Programme Statement*; Prentice-Hall International (UK) Ltd for extracts from *Principles of Marketing*, third edition by Philip Kotler; Times Newspapers Limited for extracts from the *Sunday Times* article, 'A Museum in the Pink' (17 February 1991); the United Kingdom Council for Overseas Student Affairs (UKCOSA) for extracts from their mission statement; Uxbridge College for extracts from the college mission statement.

The author wishes to thank Helen Gardiner for her transpositional skills in the preparation of the manuscript.

Every effort has been made to trace all the copyright holders, but if any have been inadvertently overlooked the publishers will make the necessary arrangement at the earliest opportunity.

1   What Is Marketing?

1.1 **Introduction**

In the private, profit-making sector, marketing arises because of the mismatch that develops between production and sales. Initial sales to an organisation's primary customers may be fairly easy to achieve, but expanding sales to less responsive customers in an increasingly competitive environment can be more difficult. This is where marketing can help, by concentrating efforts on the major customers and finding cost-effective ways of reaching the less responsive ones.

In this sense, marketing is pivotal in the processes of production and distribution. It involves a clear point of view which looks at the organisation from the customers' viewpoint and develops a series of ideas and procedures that suggest courses of action. The Chartered Institute of Marketing has defined it in the following way:

> Marketing is the management process responsible for identifying, anticipating and satisfying customer requirements profitably.

This viewpoint dates back at least as far as 1776 when Adam Smith wrote in *The Wealth of Nations*:

> Consumption is the sole end purpose of all production; and the interest of the producer ought to be attended to only in so far as it may be necessary for promoting that of the consumer.

Much more recently, Peter Drucker has defined marketing 'as the whole business seen from the point of view of its final result, that is from the customers' point of view', while Philip Kotler defines it as 'human activity directed at satisfying needs and wants through exchange processes'.

The common feature of these definitions is the satisfying of customers' needs; although this point of view is most commonly applied to industrial and commercial enterprises, it can equally be applied to any organisation that is able to identify its customers. For non-profit organisations, the Chartered Institute of Marketing's definition needs to stop at '. . . satisfying customer requirements', since profit is not the motivation. Instead, such organisations may be concerned with providing a public service and being accountable in the effective use of scarce resources (Figure 1.1). Whatever the motivation, the essential feature of marketing can be said to be an attitude of mind or point of view.

Activity 1

What do you understand by the term 'marketing' in the context of your own organisation (or one that you know well)? What activities could marketing include?

1.2 Orientation

The fundamental question for any organisation is: 'Are we product/service orientated or customer orientated?'

Product or Service Orientation
This means that an organisation produces goods or services with more concern for the production process than for consumers; it has an idea about what consumers need and produces goods to meet this viewpoint. Examples include motor car manufacturers continuing to

Fig 1.1 *Marketing exchange transactions*

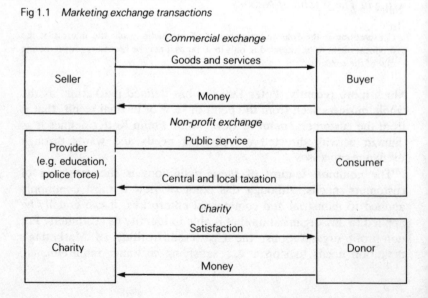

produce a model long after it has been superseded by competitors, travel companies providing the cheapest possible package holiday without any concern for quality, and computer software firms producing a program that they believe every organisation needs and should have.

In these circumstances, sales effort is based on the past reputation of the car, the price of the holiday or the brilliance of the computer program. Customer resistance is considered to be due to ignorance about the product. The focus of attention of organisations that operate in this way is on running a smooth and efficient production/distribution process. Customers have to adapt to the product and the organisation may believe that it can substantially increase the size of its market by increasing its sales effort rather than by changing the product to make it more attractive. In these circumstances, a decline in sales may be met by putting more money into advertising rather than trying to improve the product/service.

In the past, many companies were product orientated: they could sell everything they were able to produce because the demand for manufactured goods was much greater than the supply available. For example, in the late 1940s and early 1950s, there was a shortage in goods such as motor cars, so that they could be sold with a minimum of marketing. The computer boom in the 1970s and early 1980s produced similar conditions for many computer companies and their data processing programs.

Sales Orientation

In sales-orientated organisations, the main task is seen to be that of stimulating the interest of potential consumers in the existing products/services. This may involve an attempt to change consumers to fit what the company has to offer. For example, a car manufacturer may continue to try to persuade customers to buy a particular model even though the profits have fallen dramatically and market share has been shrinking for some time; travel companies may still try to sell cheap, packaged holidays even though their customers have moved on to higher quality, more expensive holidays. Such shifts in demand are often seen as temporary changes in fashion which will revert to the old position when consumers 'come to their senses'.

Customer Orientation

The main task of customer-orientated organisations is seen to be to determine the needs and wants of the customers and to satisfy them. This does not mean, however, that the organisation must cater to their every whim, or that the policy and plans of the organisation start with customer perceptions. Under these circumstances, when there is a downturn in sales or demand, an attempt is made to change the product/service to fit the consumer rather than to change the consumer to fit the product/service. For example, the quality of

Fig 1.2   *The move towards an integrated marketing organisation*

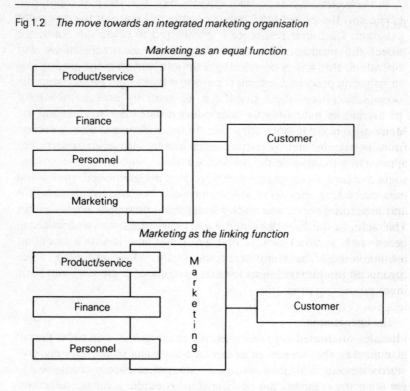

Marketing as an equal function

Marketing as the linking function

Marketing integrated in a customer-orientated organisation

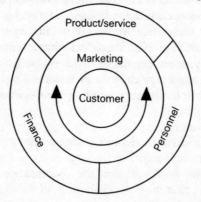

packaged holidays is improved to the level required by the holiday-makers. This means that marketing is seen as an integrated element in the functions of an organisation with the customer as the controlling element (Figure 1.2).

Activity 2

Decide whether your organisation is product/service orientated or customer orientated. List the evidence you have used to arrive at your conclusion.

Many organisations are in a transitional stage, in most cases moving from a product/service orientation towards a customer-orientated approach. In fact, even product-orientated organisations carry out some marketing in considering customer preference and in planning potential sales campaigns. This is, however, likely to be half-hearted and limited when compared to a customer-orientated organisation. The main problem may be that the organisation's products are believed to be inherently desirable, and so any lack of success is attributed to customer ignorance and a lack of motivation. In these organisations, marketing research is given a minor role and staff involved in 'marketing' activities are chosen for their product knowledge or communication skills rather than their marketing skills.

The computer software firm established on the basis of a bright idea or a specialised suite of programs or a 'niche' in the market may give marketing a very low priority because demand is generated by word of mouth and reputation, and because customers are looking for the service the firm offers. However, once the original idea has been overtaken by competitors, and demands for new ideas, the firm may decide to start marketing. This is the worst time to develop a marketing plan because it will be carried out in an atmosphere of desperation, and because profits may be falling, there will be an attempt to develop a marketing strategy at the lowest possible cost. The right time to introduce a marketing strategy is at the very beginning of the development of an organisation. Marketing is just as important when things are going well as when things are going badly: when profits are high, policies can be decided calmly. Naturally, if an organisation is doing well without a marketing strategy, the tendency will be not to introduce one. The important factor, however, is to understand why the company is successful and plan to continue this success.

1.3 The Non-profit Sector

In the public and non-profit sector, marketing has not been a traditional element in the functions of institutions and organisations. This is partly due to the fact that often the customers have been looking for the particular service on offer, and if there has been a need to generate demand, this has happened by word of mouth. However, due to changes in funding and increased competition, the public sector has become more interested in marketing, and institutions such as hospitals, schools, colleges, universities, museums, orchestras and theatres have moved into the transitional stage between product orientation and marketing (customer) orientation. Organisations such as charities and voluntary bodies have also come to realise that they must compete for donations or grants and that they need to satisfy their customers' requirements.

This trend has been most marked in public sector organisations that have been exposed to competition or may be in the future. This 'privatisation' has taken a number of forms, ranging from the sale of shares in an organisation on the stock exchange at one extreme to making an institution a 'cost-centre' at the other extreme. The first extreme means that the organisation joins the private sector and has to make a profit in order to survive. In the other extreme, the institution, such as a school or hospital, is given a level of self-government and is made responsible for its own budget. In this position, the motivation is still to provide a public service but an increased emphasis is placed on the costs at which this is provided. This may be linked to increased competition by giving the customers freedom of choice about which institution they decide to use. For example, parents may be able to choose which schools their children attend rather than having to attend the nearest one.

Public utilities, such as gas, electricity and water, and public corporations, such as telecommunications, airports and steel production, have all moved in the direction of complete privatisation. In addition, many non-profit organisations have introduced sections or programmes that are intended to be profit making: they sell goods and services to earn revenue. For example, theatres and orchestras sell tickets and subscriptions, as well as souvenir programmes and chocolates in the foyer; universities and colleges sell training courses to commerce and industry at commercial prices. However, as many profit-making organisations carry out similar activities to those provided by non-profit institutions, the latter have taken a greater interest in marketing to try to combat the increased competition; marketing can be described as 'maintaining a competitive edge'.

'Customer orientation' is a way of thinking about marketing and the whole organisation.

Activity 3

If you work in the non-profit sector, identify the marketing function in your organisation and the members of staff responsible for it.

Not many non-profit organisations put a large amount of effort into achieving customer satisfaction, but prefer to concentrate on other considerations. For example, schools and colleges may concentrate on meeting curriculum targets set by validating bodies, museums may concentrate on preserving their collections, and hospitals may concentrate on satisfying the interests of their consultants. In fact, some organisations do not want to attract any more customers so they purposely act in a way that discourages them: public utilities such as gas, electricity and water may be more interested in the sources of their products than in their customers; hospitals may not want any more patients; social security offices may not want to attract the unemployed. Such organisations may feel that they lack the budget to retrain staff towards a different way of thinking about the organisation, and they may have priorities that they believe are what the customer wants. Railway staff, for example, may believe that the only objective is for the trains to be on time and that the requirements of customer service are satisfied by this operational objective being met.

The public and non-profit sectors are not only important because of their size but also because they touch on everybody's lives. People cannot avoid using the non-profit services of the public sector, whether provided by a government department, local authority or another public agency. They are major employers, as well as being involved in all sorts of activities. The National Trust, for example, owns houses and land covering areas in all regions of the UK; charities such as OXFAM advertise widely for funds to be used mainly in Third World countries; and organisations such as the Royal National Institute for the Blind (RNIB) provide essential services such as education and specialised products.

1.4 Types of Non-profit Organisation

Non-profit organisations can be classified by the following.

Sources of funding: whether this is from government revenues through taxes and grants, from voluntary contributions or other sources.

Type of product/service: whether the organisation is producing a tangible product/service, or is concerned with a change in behaviour (anti-smoking campaigns, for example).

Organisational form:
- *donative*, in that the organisation secures its revenues mainly from donations;
- *commercial*, in that the organisation charges users for its service;
- *mutual*, in that the organisation is largely controlled by its users;
- *entrepreneurial*, in that the organisation is controlled by professional managers.

The ownership of golf clubs, for example, is often in the hands of the members but is also run on commercial lines, so can be described as *commercial/mutual*. Building societies in the UK are often commercial/mutual as well, in that they are owned by the members and charge users; they may also, at the same time, have an entrepreneurial element – that is, control by professional managers. Many religious and political organisations receive their revenue from donations and are owned by their members, and therefore are *donative/mutual*. Arts organisations and such bodies as the Red Cross can be described as *donative/entrepreneurial*, since their funds come from donations but they are controlled by professional managers.

Activity 4

How would you classify your organisation?

In fact, many public sector and non-profit organisations have divisions that can be described in different ways because they are simultaneously funded either by donations, government grants or by making charges to their customers, and may have various ways by which they are controlled. For example, the hospital shop may be run on commercial/entrepreneurial lines while the hospital itself may be based on government grants, donations and professional management. A charity, such as the RNIB, provides a service for the blind while also helping to develop products, and attempting to influence the public in its attitudes and the government in its support for blind people.

1.5 Performance Measurement of Non-profit Organisations

Public sector organisations often provide important public services that would not be otherwise available, to the same degree, on a commercial basis. These services may include: health care, social services, education and research; areas of the economic infrastructure, such as roads, railways, sewage, water, electricity, gas and so on; and local and central government services and administration, including the police force, the armed services and the administration of justice.

It can be argued that none of these services needs to be marketed, that lawful behaviour is a social requirement, that defence is a necessity and that people requiring social services will seek out the service they need. Marketing in these circumstances can be seen to be a waste of public money. Why should the police need to market themselves when they are obviously performing a public service? Should public money be spent on anti-smoking campaigns or campaigns to persuade people to wear seat belts?

One of the characteristics of the public sector is public accountability – scrutiny by a parliamentary committee or public body. Although performance may be judged largely by non-marketing measures – that is, not by profit or market share – it is judged by expenditure, efficiency targets and by the need for the service. Funding may be closely allied to such a performance measurement. In order to obtain its budget, the organisation needs the approval, or at least the acquiescence, of everybody who could be considered to be a client, customer or constituent. Where a market share of 10% may be satisfactory to a business, a 'rejection' by 90% of its 'constituents' could be fatal to a budget-based institution.

Activity 5

What quantitative indicators are used to judge your organisation? What qualitative factors would you like to be taken into account?

1.6 **Quality in the Non-profit Sector**

At the centre of marketing in the public sector is the question of quality. It is very easy to carry out a public sector service badly; in fact, it can be argued that if an organisation is not customer orientated it is likely to be doing just that. A customer-orientated organisation is one that makes every effort to sense, serve and satisfy the needs and wants of clients or customers within the constraints of its budget. The marketing approach can help an organisation to do this. For example, hospitals can make patients welcome, colleges can provide training at firms' premises and orchestras can make their music more 'accessible' by playing at lunch times at places where people congregate. This does not mean that hospitals have to lower their medical standards in order to pamper their patients. Rather, it means organising the out-patient department to meet the needs of the patient as much as that of the consultant. Educational institutions can make visitors welcome and make it easy for students to find exactly the education or training they want, without reducing educational standards. Public sector airlines can reassure customers and give them confidence in flying by the level and quality of service, without reducing the competence of their pilots.

The move towards a customer-orientated approach in organisations may be seen as an improvement on marketing decisions that were previously based on immediate profit considerations, and a consideration of society's interests in the decision-making processes may be seen as a further improvement. This approach may not appear very realistic in the private sector where the primary motivation is company survival based on profitability. The idea of worrying about the long-term problems of society may appear to be far-fetched in these circumstances. It is interesting to note, however, that many companies do take note of such interests. For example, many emphasise their use of recycled paper or other reclaimed materials, the fact that they use ozone friendly material or that they take care of the landscape. A cynical view would be that companies only pay lip-service to environmental factors in order to promote a popular image. But these interests do lead to action in some cases, such as the changes made by manufacturers of refrigerators in order to remove CFCs. The use of CFCs has been shown to have an adverse effect on the atmosphere and manufacturers have been able to replace them, thereby making their refrigerators more 'environmentally friendly'.

Non-profit organisations need to take particular care to give the correct image from the point of view of the environment and society. Their corporate objectives are less about profit and more about providing a public service. The public sector often provides services that are not profitable but which are considered desirable by policy-makers. These include education for pupils with learning difficulties, social services, provision for disadvantaged families, famine relief and so on.

Just as private sector organisations develop or acquire an image, so do those in the public sector. For example, if a police force believes that the best policy is to subdue and frighten the local population into not committing crimes, then this policy is likely to create a poor image. If, on the other hand, the police force believes that the best policy is to obtain the co-operation of the public against criminals, then the image is likely to be different. Developing the right image may improve the quality and the efficiency of the service that the police force can provide. The Metropolitan Police, for example, in its document *A Common Purpose for the 1990s* states that it 'has a strong tradition of service to the public and our common purpose must now be to make the quality of that service even better'.

Activity 6

Why should the chief consultant of a hospital, the chief executive of a large charity or the principal of a college be interested in marketing?

1.7 Marketing and the Environment

It can be argued that the 'pure' concept of marketing may conflict with political and social objectives concerned with environmental deterioration, resource shortage, population growth, neglected social services and ideas about the 'quality of life'. Maintaining a competitive edge may not be seen to be in the best interests of consumers and society. There may be a conflict between immediate consumer wants and long-term consumer welfare.

In the private sector, the proper goal of marketing may be considered to be to maximise consumption, which will help to create maximum production, employment and wealth. By maximising choice and enabling customers to find goods that precisely satisfy their tastes, it can be argued that companies are improving the customers' life style and, therefore, their satisfaction. It is easy to measure consumer satisfaction in terms of demand – that is, by the value of their purchases; it is much more difficult when attempts are made to measure consumer satisfaction factors such as pollution and environmental damage and concepts such as the 'quality of life'. For example, for a few people to wear fur coats now may mean the extinction of certain species of animals in the future; the packaging of products in easily handled aerosols for some people may lead to environmental damage for all.

There is an increased recognition that 'responsible' marketing should be concerned with the quality of life, not only in terms of the quality, quantity, range, accessibility and cost of goods, but also in the quality of the physical and cultural environment. There is public support for government campaigns for energy conservation, against smoking, against drinking and driving, and about AIDS. These are marketing campaigns concerned with the quality of life; they are attempts to 'sell' ideas and information to the public. An anti-smoking campaign, for example, is an attempt to sell an idea to smokers and potential smokers. The effectiveness of the campaign will depend on how persuasive it is and how well it is aimed at the target audience.

1.8 Marketing and Selling

Although marketing and selling overlap, they are two different activities. Selling is the point at which an exchange is agreed between supplier and customer. Marketing is the whole process directed at satisfying needs and wants through exchange. Selling can be seen as the culmination of this process, which is most likely to succeed when the elements of marketing have been well organised.

The marketing process comprises:

• finding out what the customer wants;
• developing products/services to satisfy these wants;
• establishing a price consistent with the requirements of the supplier and the perceptions of the customer;
• distributing products/services to the customer;
• agreeing on the exchange – selling.

At the point of sale, the objective is to persuade the customer to take the step from wanting a product/service to buying it. Although some goods will 'sell themselves' and customers will actively seek out these goods or services, in most circumstances this is not the case. The more closely the commodity or service matches the customers' needs, the easier it will be to clinch the sale, and this is more likely to happen when an organisation is marketing (customer) orientated than when it is not.

The whole purpose of marketing is to provide a product/service that matches the customers' needs. Even organisations that do not have a marketing department carry out some marketing function: it may be disguised in the form of product design, advertising and promotion, or customer service. For example, popular theatre productions such as 'The Phantom of the Opera' may need little marketing or promotion after the initial successful launch but some marketing effort will have been undertaken during the months leading up to the launch.

The main difference between marketing and selling arises out of the understanding that customers are not looking for products/ services, but are looking for benefits (Figure 1.3). In the case of customers looking for entertainment, the satisfaction of this requirement can be in a variety of forms. The managers of a theatre, for example, need to persuade customers that they can satisfy their need by attending a performance of 'The Phantom of the Opera'.

When a consumer buys a loaf of bread the basic need is not for bread but to satisfy hunger. In a wealthy society, it is possible to satisfy this need without eating bread, a fact that bakers need to understand when trying to sell their product. In the UK, this is a lesson that butchers have had to learn very quickly because although the demand to satisfy hunger has not diminished, the demand for meat as a way of achieving this has diminished in recent years.

Fig 1.3   *Selling and marketing compared*

	Focus	**Method**	**Results**
Private sector			
Selling	Products	Selling/promoting	Profits through sales volume
Marketing	Customers' needs	Integrated marketing	Profits through customer satisfaction
Non-profit sector			
Selling	Services	Selling/promoting	Accountability based on volume
Marketing	Customers' needs	Integrated marketing	Accountability based on customer satisfaction

Activity 7

Identify the differences between marketing and selling as applied to your own organisation. Who has the main responsibility for selling?

The benefits that people seek from the police force are security and peace of mind, and an absence of crime. The strategies and techniques used to achieve these benefits will be accepted in so far as they appear to be achieving these benefits. In a similar fashion, a patient entering hospital for an operation is seeking the benefit of good health and has accepted that hospital treatment is the way to achieve it.

This view of organisations suggests that they should make or provide what can be sold rather than sell what can be made. The marketing concept holds here that the most important action is to determine the needs and wants of the target market and to deliver the desired satisfactions more effectively and efficiently than competitors. The selling concept focuses on the needs of the seller, while marketing focuses on the needs of the buyer. Selling is preoccupied with the seller's needs to convert the product into cash, while marketing is concerned with the idea of satisfying the needs of the customer by means of the product/service. The selling concept starts with the company's existing product and looks for intense promotion to achieve profitable sales. The marketing concept starts with the needs and wants of the company's target customers, and the company achieves its profits through creating and maintaining customer satisfaction.

While the idea of selling assumes inertia and resistance on the part of the consumer, the idea of marketing is to make selling as superfluous as possible by knowing and understanding the consumer so that the product/service sells itself. Ideally, marketing will result in a consumer that is ready to buy so that all that is needed is for the product/service to be available.

1.9 Conclusion

An organisation that is product/service orientated (whether it is in the private or public sector) may still carry out marketing functions, but they are likely to be half-hearted and limited compared with those of an organisation dedicated to marketing. The 'culture' and 'attitude' of two such organisations will be at opposite ends of the product marketing spectrum, with many organisations in a transitional stage between them.

A fully integrated marketing orientation will permeate the whole structure of an organisation. In the private sector, profits will continue to be fundamental to business survival but they will be obtained by the organisation satisfying the customer. In the non-profit sector, results may be difficult to measure because they are intangible or long term, so that a school or college, for example, may improve the education of its pupils or students but this may be difficult to prove. This problem, combined with an increasing emphasis on accountability, may lead to a situation where what is measurable may become the priority. For example, if the only criterion of success for a school is examination results, then this may become the sole objective, so that more general educational objectives may be forgotten. The other problem with non-profit organisations is that they may become mainly concerned with the size of their budget. Success may be measured by the size of the budget, so that a prime objective will be to spend it fully each year so that there is no apparent reason to reduce it.

Marketing is the idea or concept that an organisation's decisions should be governed by its market and its customers, rather than by its technical facilities. It is an orderly, systematic process of business planning, execution and control. It is directed at influencing the level, training and character of demand in a way that will help the organisation to achieve its objectives, whether these are related to making a profit or providing a public service.

1.10 Case Study

A charity will market to its donors and the general public. 'Marketing' will mean the importance of a good image and a high reputation for the efficiency and effectiveness of its management, and the ability to help the cause or causes with which it is concerned.

A charity may be product orientated in the sense that its management believes it knows what the donors and the recipients of the charity want. There may be details of how the charity will spend its money, but these will be mainly directed at the management efficiency of the organisation rather than the needs of the recipients.

In contrast, a marketing-orientated charity will not only seek to be efficient but will also actively seek the views of its donors and recipients when possible: a charity for the blind can ask blind people what they want while a charity for animals cannot ask for the views of its recipients, but it can spend its money for the sake of the animals and not for unnecessary bureaucracy. Marketing may mean public relations, marketing research and care. The overall image of the charity will depend on the cause it is supporting and the image the public has of this. Much will depend on the people working for the charity, both full-time and part-time workers; that is, the people directly involved with the donors and the recipients. Some charities employ marketing or public relations specialists but they will still depend heavily on the work of the paid and voluntary staff.

A charity receives most of its income from donors with the objective that the money raised will be spent on the declared objective of the charity in the best possible way.

A charity will emphasise the results of its work, whether this is with the objective of relieving famine, providing for the disabled or carrying out research into an illness. It will also report on the proportion of its money spent on administration as against the proportion spent on its main objectives. A charity will want qualitative results taken into account to show the success it has had in, for example, improving the quality of life of the recipients of its services.

The chief executive of a charity should be interested in marketing because it is through this activity that money is raised and the objectives of the charity are realised. The chief executive can provide leadership in achieving the objectives through a range of activities, which together can be seen as part of the marketing effort.

This culminates in the 'point of sale', which in a charity is the point at which donors contribute money to the charity. Responsibility for the 'sale' will depend on paid and voluntary staff dealing directly with the public and through other marketing activities such as advertising.

2 The Marketing Activity

2.1 The Need for Marketing

Traditionally, marketing has been linked to the concepts of profitability and of providing a competitive edge. It is sensible, therefore, to ask what the role of marketing is in an organisation where profit is not the motive and where retaining a competitive edge may not be of primary importance.

The essential link is the idea of customer service. Non-profit organisations provide services or, in some instances, products for people who may be variously described as consumers, customers, clients, patients, passengers or 'the public'. Marketing involves a mutually beneficial exchange between the producer and the consumer. In a commercial company, this is reasonably straightforward: the company produces a product/service, the consumer pays for it and the company has the objective of making a profit from this transaction. Exchange relationships in non-profit organisations are more complicated, since they may be influenced by statutory and other requirements. A product/service is provided but the consumer may not be asked to pay for it, so the organisation will not have the objective of making a profit.

Activity 1

'There are many similarities between running a business and running a public authority, but there are also some crucial differences' (John Harvey-Jones). What do you think are the crucial differences?

Although there are differences between the profit and non-profit sectors, there are two fundamental concepts of marketing that are common to both: the idea of customer service and the idea of a mutually beneficial exchange. Some of the services provided by one sector can, in fact, be equally well provided by the other sector. This includes many central and local government services, products and services produced by nationalised industry, the services of arts associations and similar organisations, and perhaps even the services provided by some charities and voluntary bodies. Whether, for example, people catch a bus that is run by the local authority, a public transport board or by a private company is unimportant to the passenger, who may not realise, and usually does not need to know, who owns the organisation involved. The passenger is concerned with the efficiency of the service and the price of the ticket, and will only need to find out who is responsible for the bus when making a complaint. In this case, the consumer has a need to travel at a cost that can be afforded and this need may be satisfied equally well by the public or the private sector.

Activity 2

How is payment made for the products/services produced by your organisation? What proportion is direct payment and what proportion indirect?

In the same way, when a customer buys a car from a showroom the fact that it has been produced by a company that is heavily subsidised by government may not be known or felt to be an important part of the decision about which car to buy. Some of the services provided by some charities, for example old people's homes, could be financed by a local authority or sponsored by a private company. For the old people, it is the service that they receive which is important.

It is interesting to note that public sector organisations have marketed themselves for many years although they may describe these activities by a different name. Political parties, for example, publicise themselves and their candidates, particularly at election times; governments often have offices of information to communicate their policies and to support campaigns on particular issues such as drinking and driving, smoking, drug use, AIDS; local authorities advertise their leisure centres and other amenities; and charities campaign for funds.

Marketing is needed in the public sector because people require information about a service; they want to know what is available, when and where it is available, and whether or not there is a direct charge (Figure 2.1). This need for marketing has been given a sharper focus by pressure to use public resources efficiently, effectively and economically; in general, the non-profit sector has become increasingly accountable for its use of money and for the quality of its

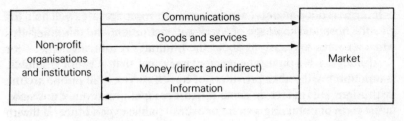

Fig 2.1 *The marketing structure*

performance in providing services. This accountability is expressed in terms of performance indicators or by public reaction rather than in terms of profit, which again results in more complex relationships than those that tend to exist in the private sector.

Activity 3

What do you consider to be the role of marketing in the non-profit sector? List the main differences you can identify between this role and the role of marketing in the profit-making sector.

A school, for example, will be accountable to its governing body, local authority officers and members, advisors, and central and local government inspectors as well as parents. They all have a right to ask about the school's performance in terms of examination results or the number of school-leavers obtaining jobs or progressing to higher education. They may also want to know about staffing levels, the availability of resources and how money has been spent. The input into the school is central and local government money; the output is well-educated pupils.

What is meant by 'well educated' is, of course, more open to question and discussion than what is meant by 'profit', so that performance indicators (such as examination results), which may be concerned with 'quality' and 'cost effectiveness', are complicated by the need to interpret their meaning.

In a similar way, a national health hospital provides a service to its patients, perhaps without any real competition. This service can be provided well or badly so that, for example, out-patients may wait for long periods in uncomfortable surroundings or may have an efficient appointment system and an attractive waiting room. As well as helping to reduce anxiety, a well-organised reception area will help to give the hospital the image of a well-run institution, and this may help when it comes to decisions about the hospital's resourcing.

Although a hospital management may feel that it is not in direct competition with other providers of health services, all public sector institutions are, in fact, in some form of competition, even if it is only in the form of obtaining a share of overall public expenditure. If there is a limited amount of money to be allocated to hospitals nationally or regionally, the reputation of a hospital may be important in determining the share it obtains.

Many public services are provided 'free' in the sense that the consumer does not pay directly for the service at the time of receiving it. It may be felt that if price is not involved in a transaction and competition is limited, marketing is not required. However, all products and services have to be paid for in one way or another, and the consumer will normally do this, even if it is by a very indirect route as a taxpayer (see Figure 2.2). The common denominator is customer service in both profit and non-profit organisations. The 'free' local authority leisure centre, for instance, will be unlikely to continue in operation if it is not used; the 'free' or subsidised bus service will soon be curtailed if the buses are empty.

Activity 4

To whom is your organisation accountable? What does this mean in practice?

Services have to provide what consumers want, when they want it. If people are queuing up for a service, then either they are receiving what they want or there is no competition; in these circumstances, marketing will be seen to be unimportant. This is, of course, just as true in the private sector as in the public sector. Many profit-making companies are product orientated because there is a constant profitable demand for their product and they do not, therefore, feel the need to put any effort into marketing. The risk is that when a company finds its profit declining it will not have developed the marketing infrastructure to halt this decline. A number of information technology companies, for example, have found themselves in this situation because they were founded on the basis of technical expertise for which there appeared to be an inexhaustible demand, so that when competitors flooded the market they had not developed the marketing skills to resist the new challenges and retain the competitive edge.

Survival is the most important goal in most organisations, even if this is not spelt out in mission statements and corporate objectives. The financial battles surrounding take-over bids tend to support this view, as do industrial battles over the future of trade unions and political battles over the future of public institutions. Organisations provide security for their workforce whereas a major change brings uncertainty. The survival of an organisation is much easier if the marketing approach has already been established before threats have developed, because marketing can help to make the most of the strengths of an organisation in order to meet the challenge of competition.

Activity 5

Identify the factors that determine the 'survival' of your organisation. Can marketing help in this process?

2.2 Who Are the Customers?

Non-profit organisations have to identify their customers if they are to improve customer services. In most situations, identification is straightforward: in the private sector the customer is the person who pays for the product/service; in the public sector the customer is the person who receives the service whether there is a direct payment or an indirect one (through taxation). It is usually obvious who is receiving the public service in the case of bus services, leisure centres, theatres, hospitals, schools and nationalised industries. There are, however, organisations such as charities and arts associations where identification of the client may be less obvious.

All organisations have customers at various levels and there may be a number of layers between the producer and the final consumer. Wholesalers are customers of manufacturing companies and have retailers as their customers. It can be argued, of course, that both the wholesaler and the retailer are in fact consumers of the goods they receive but not the 'final' consumer. In practice, it is very difficult to distinguish between the various terms used, such as 'customer', 'consumer' or 'client', and it is often more a question of custom and practice in a particular organisation, industry or public service.

Activity 6

Identify exactly who are the customers of your organisation.

Most organisations need to market in more than one direction because the people who pay for and/or receive the service may not be the only people who have an interest in it. There are people and bodies who determine whether or not, and how much, an organisation receives in income and investment. These bodies may be holding companies, a board of directors, a governing body, a local authority, central government, or some other group, board or council. The people involved may or may not be consumers of the service, but they are concerned with the efficiency and effectiveness of the organisation and the quality of its customer service, so that the performance of the organisation will be one of the factors which determine the amount of money allocated to it (Figure 2.2).

Activity 7

What do you understand by internal marketing? To whom do you need to market internally?

Internal reports and presentations to persuade people that money should be allocated in one direction rather than another are typical of all large organisations and are a very important feature of the non-profit sector where income is frequently in the form of a grant or budget allocation. Many public sector organisations need to influence local authorities, central government, industrial companies or other bodies in order to obtain income. Universities, for example, receive their income from a variety of sources, including a central government funding body, research councils, sponsorship from industry, tuition fees from individuals or via local authority grants. These groups are not necessarily all consumers; most of them are more like shareholders who need to be convinced that they are making a sound investment.

In the same way, a hospital's clients are its patients, but the management needs to influence not only them but also the regional hospital board and the government. The two factors may be linked, because satisfied patients may have an important influence on public funding. A school needs to consider the local authority as well as its

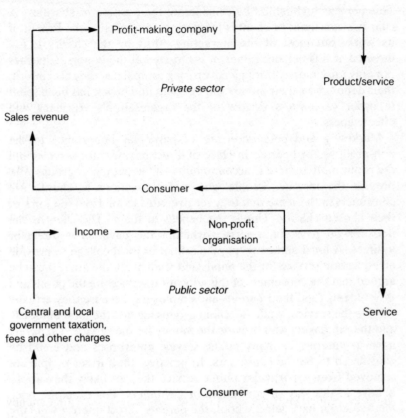

Fig 2.2 *Private and public sector exchange relationships*

pupils and their parents; the police have to consider its image with local and central government as well as the public.

Activity 8

'The Government channels money into the health service through 24 English and Welsh regional health authorities who then have the job of deciding how much each district health authority should get .... In 1984 ... the Chairman of the Regional Health Authority ... struck a bargain with Shropshire: if the county could find savings worth half the running costs of the new hospital at Telford, the region would finance the other half ' (John Harvey-Jones). Are you aware of any such 'bargains' arranged by your organisation?

This point is highlighted by considering the position of charities. A charity's consumer or client is the person who receives the benefit of its work, but most of the marketing effort by the charity is not directed at this person; rather, it is targeted at the donors. Charities not only raise money through advertising campaigns, they also inform their donors how their money will be spent and how it has been spent in order to impress donors of the organisation's efficiency and effectiveness.

Marketing and persuasion are of particular importance to the non-profit sector because in place of direct payment for services and the profit motive there is accountability to the people or groups who provide the income. People who make donations to charity are consumers in the sense that they receive satisfaction from the work of their chosen charity. This is the benefit to them. The client is the person who pays for a service whether the payment is direct or indirect. A local authority 'pays' a school or local college to provide an education service for the pupils and students in the area. It can be argued that the consumers of this education service are the pupils and the students (and their parents and employers) because they actually receive the service, while the client groups include the local authority and the ratepayers who provide the money for the service. Taxpayers have an interest in many public service enterprises and could be considered to be the consumers. In practice, the further people are removed from a particular public service the less likely they are to behave in the way of consumers or customers. For example, once their children have left a school, the parents' direct interest will fade very quickly.

2.3 The Importance of Marketing Orientation

In the past, the public sector has been largely product orientated. Hospitals, schools and local authorities have tended to adopt the attitude that they provide a service and people are welcome to come and receive it. Just as commercial firms have had to move from a product orientation to a marketing orientation since the 1950s, so public sector and non-profit bodies have been encouraged to move in the same direction in recent years.

The acceptance of this objective in many non-profit organisations has meant that the debate has moved not from *whether* they should be more marketing orientated but to *how* they can achieve this objective. In most cases, the model adopted is that of manufacturing industry, since the marketing function is clearly illustrated when considering the production and selling of cars or packets of crisps.

However, there are fundamental differences between this model and the non-profit sector: in manufacturing industry the marketing activity tends to concentrate on the external environment, while in public sector and non-profit organisations the internal environment and organisational structure may be key factors in the marketing activity, although the external environment is just as important.

Many public and non-profit institutions provide services that are labour intensive (such as schools, colleges, universities, hospitals and old people's homes) and there is considerable interaction between the staff of these institutions and the consumers of their services (teachers and pupils, lecturers and students, doctors/nurses and patients), which makes the producer–consumer interaction crucial. In these circumstances, institutional and management development of the marketing activity is essential to provide support for staff and to develop customer–conscious personnel (Figure 2.3).

The establishment of a separate marketing department or unit may be appropriate when the product being sold is a commodity that the consumer can learn about through advertising or by seeing it on display in shops, for example. Under these conditions, the production staff may not need to have any conception of the marketing process.

In conclusion, where a non-profit organisation provides a service, marketing needs to permeate every layer of the organisation if it is to have a genuine marketing orientation as opposed to window dressing. The greater the participation and involvement of staff in promoting the image and direction of the organisation the greater will be their commitment, motivation and level of productivity.

2.4 Creating the Right Image

Marketing in the non-profit sector often concentrates on image and reputation. The image of an organisation is an intangible factor that reflects the views that outsiders have of it and the quality of its service. A school, for example, may have a reputation for good or bad behaviour, excellent or poor examination results, or high or low calibre staff, which may or may not be deserved. While the school is full, its image may not matter, but once the school begins to have spare places, either because it has expanded or the number of pupils has fallen, the situation changes and the school needs to attract pupils. To do this, the school managers attempt to establish a good reputation and image for their school. However, it is difficult to establish a good reputation quickly and it is a little late to try to do this when the need becomes fully apparent. It is when the school is

Marketing a product in the profit-making sector

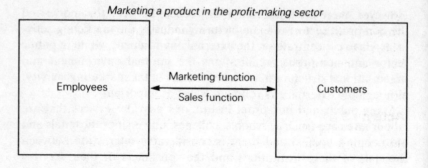

Marketing a service in the profit-making sector

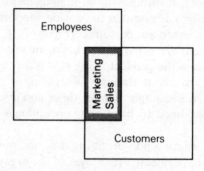

Marketing a service in the non-profit sector

Fig 2.3　*Employee–customer links*

full that the good image needs to be created.

The image of an organisation is the set of beliefs, ideas and impressions that people have of it. Once an image has been established, it is often difficult to change it because people tend to be selective about any further information they receive, and may believe what they want to believe rather than looking closely at the facts. This makes it even more important for non-profit organisations to become 'image conscious'.

Activity 9

How would you describe the reputation and 'image' of your organisation? What image do you have of:

- your local primary school;
- your local authority;
- British Rail;
- your nearest hospital;
- Oxfam;
- CND?

How do you think you have formed your opinions of these institutions?

The image of a school or hospital will be greatly influenced by customers' perceptions, which will depend on what they hear about the institution as well as any service they receive from it. The parent, child or patient will receive information in a number of ways, some of which will be haphazard, such as talking to friends, reading the odd piece of news in the local paper, passing the buildings of the institution, or seeing pupils or patients emerging from it. If a school or hospital wants to create an image of an efficient, caring institution it will need to consider all the ways that people receive information and make sure that it is not haphazard and that it includes information that the institution wants people to receive. If the only reports in the local paper are about things going wrong in the institution, this is likely to create a negative image. The school or hospital management can help to promote a more positive image by informing the local press about all the good things that happen at the school or hospital and the successes that are achieved. Perhaps the buildings can be brightened up, the grounds kept tidy and in good order, signposts erected that are clear and helpful, and the reception made cheerful as well as efficient.

2.5 Influences on Consumer Behaviour

The customers of non-profit organisations consist of all the individuals, households, companies and other groups who buy or acquire their goods or services for consumption. These consumers will vary greatly in age, income, educational level, mobility and tastes. It may be useful to distinguish different client groups and to develop services tailored to their needs, and if a market segment is large enough, an organisation may set up special marketing programmes to serve it.

The questions that need to be asked in any organisation are: who buys the service, how, when and why do they buy, and how do they respond to various market stimuli? On the one hand, the consumer may be stimulated by the environment: the state of the economy, developments in technology, the political climate, cultural influences; on the other hand, the market stimuli consist of product, price, place and promotion (the four 'Ps'), and the way these are combined or 'mixed' to make a more or less attractive product/service. Customers have needs and marketing is directed at meeting them. This is as true for non-profit organisations as for those in the private sector, and their promotion and image can be geared towards this.

Maslow's 'hierarchy of needs' suggests a list of people's needs rising from hunger and thirst to self-development:

- self-actualisation (self-development);
- esteem needs (self-esteem, recognition);
- social needs (sense of belonging);
- safety needs (security);
- physiological needs (hunger and thirst).

Non-profit organisations provide for many of the most basic of these needs. Central and local authority services, such as the provision of social security or meals on wheels, can be linked to hunger and thirst, and a public board may provide the water supply; the police force and armed services can be linked to the need for protection and security; health services can be linked with security; social services are linked to a sense of belonging; and education is concerned with a sense of belonging, self-esteem, recognition, self-development and self-realisation. Many charities are concerned with the provision of food, health services or support for social needs, as well as perhaps providing self-esteem for the donors.

Once the physiological needs have been satisfied, other needs will become important. Education, for example, may not be the most fundamental of needs because it is not directly linked to hunger and thirst, but in developing countries it is viewed as a very high priority because there is a clear link between education and better living standards. Whether a public service is seen as a necessity or a luxury will affect the way in which it is marketed. For example, people view health care as a necessity and they will seek it out irrespective of positive marketing; on the other hand, the services of a leisure centre may be thought of as a luxury, and so the centre will need to promote itself.

Activity 10

Draw a diagram (perhaps a flow chart) to show how the customers of your organisation make decisions about buying or demanding its goods/services.

The ability of a non-profit organisation to meet its customers' needs is not based on the usual economic factors of supply, demand and price. The quality of the school, hospital, prison or old people's home will depend on the resources made available as a result of political and social factors, as well as economic considerations, and will depend on how efficiently the resources are used. While there are some similarities in the influences on customer behaviour between profit and non-profit organisations, there are also clear differences, so that while general principles can be applied, detailed differences need to be considered.

2.6 Marketing in the Non-profit Sector

The need for marketing in the non-profit sector arises from the importance of the quality of the service and how far it meets the needs of the consumers. A high quality service is likely to be perceived as useful, efficient and worthy of attracting continued funding. Organisations such as schools, hospitals, police forces and charities have to carry out marketing research to find out what the public wants and then try to provide it as well as possible, given the resources available. They then need to publicise what they can provide, so that people know what they are doing and that they are doing it well.

All of these functions are marketing activities. The local sports centre or the local library has to publicise its facilities to encourage people to use them. Feedback from customers and users, whether in the form of encouragement or complaints, may result in changes in the facilities in order to meet the public's needs. The quality of the service is what the consumer is concerned about. The difference in terms of marketing various organisations may be more in the minds of the members of an organisation rather than in the minds of the public. The concept of marketing in labour-intensive, consumer-orientated organisations is a corporate affair involving everybody working for the organisation. The concept involves:

- customer orientation;
- organisational integration and cohesion;
- mutually beneficial exchange between the consumer and the organisation.

It can be argued that local authorities, for example, are in existence to provide services to the public and that marketing as a customer-orientated technique assists the authorities to determine their objectives and to assess priorities for their resources. The service provided is only of real value if it is of value to those people who receive it. Local authorities do in fact relate to target markets, such as social services (old people's homes), education (various types of schools), recreation (special concessions for the unemployed). However, they suffer from a limited availability of resources which results in an even greater need to establish priorities and to ensure that resources are allocated in the most appropriate way. Although these priorities are established on a political basis, factual information from the market can ease the decision-making process.

Activity 11

List the main marketing activities carried out by your organisation.

Marketing is a continuous process. In local authorities and other public and non-profit organisations, monitoring and review of this process is an important aspect of a marketing plan.

In conclusion, it can be said that marketing is that function of an organisation in the public and non-profit sector that can keep in constant touch with the organisation's consumers, assess their needs, develop services and products that meet these needs, and build a programme of communications to express the organisation's purpose.

2.7 Case Study

The general management skills required in a profit-making organisation and a non-profit organisation are very similar. Skills are required in human resource management, in product/service planning and control, in public relations and marketing, and in finance. However, the priorities, as well as the levels of responsibility and accountability, will be different in the two organisations. The headteacher of a secondary school will have priorities in terms of the pupils and staff, and the maintenance of the buildings and equipment, as much as with finance. The ability of the headteacher to make decisions quickly and to 'get things done' may be more limited than that of the manager in a profit-making organisation because the layers of control and public accountability are likely to be greater.

A secondary school in the public/state sector will receive most of its income from the local education authority and/or from central government; it may raise a comparatively small amount of money from parents and other sources, such as local employers. In the private sector, a school may still be non-profit making but most of the income will come from fees, paid by parents and from endowments, and other money from benefactors.

Both types of school will have areas of direct payment, such as the school 'tuck shop' and charges made for organised trips and holidays. The proportion of direct payment will be much greater in the private sector school, perhaps close to 100%, than in the state sector school, where it may be less than 2%.

Marketing in the state secondary school will be concentrated on its image and reputation based on high quality teaching/learning. The service provided by the school is in terms of 'education', but the main measure of successful product/service design, marketing and selling is not profit, as it is in the profit-making sector. A private 'crammer' may rely just as much on profit as on examination results to judge its success, and so marketing will be essential in order to maintain a competitive edge.

A state secondary school will be accountable to its governors, the local education authority and/or central government, as well as to its parents and pupils. In practice, this means parents' meetings, governing body control of policy and aspects of management, and local authority and/or central government control of the overall budget and a demand for statistical information and the inspection of quality.

The school will 'survive' as long as pupils continue to attend in sufficient numbers and it is supported by the local education authority and/or central government. Marketing to pupils and parents, as well as to the local education authority and/or central government, can help to maintain and improve pupil numbers and support.

The customers of the secondary school are the pupils and their parents. The pupils will receive the service of the school while the parents will pay for the service, directly or indirectly, and will decide, certainly for younger pupils, which school their children should attend.

The local authority and/or central government are also customers because they are the more direct paymasters. The local employers and centres of further and higher education can also be considered as customers because they employ or receive the pupils of the school.

The groups that work within the school, such as pupils, staff and governors, need to have a good image of the school so that they can give positive information externally. This is where internal marketing is important – that is, telling these groups about results, activities and events about which the school can be proud.

Schools can arrange 'bargains' with employers as well as local and/or central government. Employers provide resources, such as computers and sports equipment, in return for publicity. Development funding is occasionally provided by central government, providing the school raises part of the funds required.

People's opinions of a secondary school are formed by:

- 'word of mouth' – that is, what other children, parents and neighbours say about it;
- examination results;
- sporting achievements;
- the appearance of the school;
- the uniform;
- how well children they know have done;
- anecdotal 'evidence'.

A secondary school's customers, parents and pupils will decide to choose one school rather than another based on a number of factors. These can include the location of the school, its reputation, its facilities and so on. Pupils of eleven years of age, for example, together with their parents, will have to make a decision based on the information provided by the local authority and/or the schools. Knowledge of this process will help a school to decide when and how to provide the information and the matters that need to be emphasised. For example, if location is a problem and parents are worried about their children travelling long distances, the school can highlight the efficient coach service it operates.

A list of marketing activities for a secondary school may include:

- open days;
- parents' evenings;
- publicity events and public relations;
- publications;
- liaison with other schools, employers and colleges;
- encouragement of staff and pupils to think and speak highly of the school.

3 The Marketing Plan

3.1 What Business Are We in?

Non-profit organisations are often as product/service orientated as any private company. For example, universities and colleges produce lists of long established courses in prospectuses which tend to be handbooks for the staff of the institution rather than a marketing vehicle directed at potential students. Many of these courses are delivered in a way that best suits the needs of the institution rather than those of the client and customer.

In the same way that marketing may be given low priority in a private firm because it may not be viewed as a direct factor in the profit-making process, so it is the case when college and university students have to queue up for courses and the main purpose of the institution is seen as 'teaching' or 'research'. Public sector organisations may consider that their service and the administration and finance that support it are as important as production, sales and profit are to private sector organisations.

It can be argued that an organisation identifies marketing as important once it begins to ask what 'line of business' it is actually in. But this question needs to be linked to customer benefits: 'What benefit does our customer seek?' For example, the customer who wants to remove the branch of a tree is not concerned with how it is removed, providing the desired end is achieved effectively and cheaply without unpleasant side-effects. Using a saw may be the obvious solution. However, if a simple cut in the bark followed by an injection would have the same effect at the same price, saws might go out of use. Thus, saw producers need to realise that, among other things, they are in the branch removal business to keep up with product developments.

The Frazer–Nash Consultancy Ltd has a well-focused idea of its market and its objectives, as set out in Figure 3.1. In the same way, universities and colleges need to be very clear about the business they are in. Are they providing a menu of courses for people to pick and choose, or are they in the 'learning' business, helping people to learn skills and techniques, and acquire knowledge? If research is con-

Frazer–Nash Consultancy provides high quality engineering consultancy services to a large range of industries.

Mission statement

Our mission is:

To be a leading engineering consultancy engaged in the management and execution of projects requiring the effective application of engineering technologies and physical sciences.

We believe that:

- Our reputation depends on our quality and integrity – we are committed to achieving high standards.
- Nothing is perfect and therefore everything can and should be improved.
- Promises must be honoured, particularly price, specification and delivery.
- Our customers pay our salaries, and are therefore important.
- People matter.
- Collectively, teams can generally accomplish more than the sum of the contributions of individuals.
- We cannot provide a high quality service unless we are financially viable. Conservation of cash is therefore equally as important as technical excellence, delivery on time and profitability.
- We must value and support our suppliers.

Therefore the objectives are:

For clients and customers: A high standard of service and products which represent good value for their cost.

For suppliers and subcontractors: A reasonable profit and fair terms of trade.

For the nation: A fair contribution to the Treasury by way of taxation and to the Bank of England by way of foreign currency arising from exports and an enhanced reputation of quality and performance.

For shareholders: A reasonable return on their capital, commensurate with the risks involved.

For staff: A safe, healthy, secure, interesting and well-rewarding working environment.

Fig 3.1   *Company mission statement and objectives of the Frazer–Nash Consultancy*

cerned with pushing back the frontiers of human knowledge, then that is the criterion against which it may be judged. A university research programme may be better judged on this basis than on the number of people involved, the size of laboratories or some other concrete measure.

The question 'What is our business?' has to be defined in terms of the underlying need that the organisation is trying to serve. A hospital, for example, may be trying to serve the health needs of the local community. The benefits being sought are in terms of good health, or freedom from ill-health. This overall objective or 'mission statement' can be put into sharper focus by considering the role of the organisation in terms of:

1. Who is to be served? Which consumer groups?
2. What benefits are to be delivered? Which consumer needs are to be satisfied?
3. How are consumers to be satisfied? What technologies are to be employed?

3.2 The Mission Statement

The mission statement of an organisation describes its basic purpose. A railway company may describe itself as being in the transportation business; a computer company may describe itself as providing low cost, high quality solutions to business problems; a retail company may describe itself as offering customers a range of high quality, well-designed and attractive merchandise at reasonable prices. In the same way, a hospital can describe its purpose as providing high quality health care to its patients within the local community; a college may describe itself as providing a full range of high quality further and continuing education and training (Figure 3.2).

The point about all these mission statements is that they are succinct, distinctive and wide in scope. They are 'short in numbers and long in rhetoric' in the sense that they identify the organisation without providing a very specific and limiting approach for dealing with a target market.

The mission statement should outline the current stance of the organisation and suggest possible future intentions. It should be feasible, motivating and distinctive but not restrictive. The National Children's Bureau states, for example, that it 'exists to promote and

Fig 3.2   *College mission statement*

> At Uxbridge College, we strive to be an effective and caring organisation committed to providing a full range of further and continuing education and training of the highest quality to meet the needs of all individuals and employers in the local and wider communities.

protect the welfare, interests and rights of all children in the UK, on the basis of research and knowledge'.

Activity 1

'The non-profit organisation exists to bring about a change in individuals and in society. Its product is a changed human being. The non-profit institutions are human change-agents. Their "product" is a cured patient, a child that learns . . .' (Peter Drucker). How do these statements reflect on your organisation? Does it have a mission statement or general goals or objectives that bring out these points?

The computer company may want to emphasise the fact that it concentrates on solving business problems and that it is not in the games or toy business; the retail company may want to emphasise high quality rather than low cost; the hospital may want to limit its area of work to a well-defined locality; the college may want to make it clear that it is in the further and continuing education sector and not in higher education.

The mission statement establishes a clear view of the area of work of the organisation or institution and its aspirations in terms of quality or design or costs. The Statement of Common Purpose of the Metropolitan Police set out in Figure 3.3 is an illustration of this.

Fig 3.3　*Statement of Common Purpose of the Metropolitan Police*

The Metropolitan Police emphasises the fact that the public pay over £1 billion each year for the policing of London and they have every right to expect a cost-effective service. Their 'Statement of Common Purpose and Motives for the 1990s' (or mission statement) states:

'The purpose of the Metropolitan Police Service is to uphold the law fairly and firmly; to prevent crime; to pursue and bring to justice those who break the law; to keep the Queen's Peace; to protect, help and reassure people in London; and to be seen to do all this with integrity, common sense and sound judgement.

We must be compassionate, courteous and patient, acting without fear or favour or prejudice to the rights of others. We need to be professional, calm and restrained in the face of violence, and apply only that force which is necessary to accomplish our lawful duty.

We must strive to reduce the fears of the public and, so far as we can, to reflect their priorities in the action we take. We must respond to well-founded criticism with a willingness to change.'

Activity 2

What are your views on the mission statements given in Figures 3.1, 3.2, 3.3 and 3.5? How far do they assist you in your understanding of the purpose of the institutions to which they refer?

3.3 Corporate Objectives

The corporate objectives of an organisation emphasise a major variable such as profitability, market share or reputation. In the non-profit sector, this might be in terms of student numbers in a

Fig 3.4 *Educational objectives*

The education committee therefore calls for a commitment by all concerned in the education service in Cheshire to the following aims and objectives:

- To operate and develop a system of education which is capable of identifying and meeting the educational needs of children, young people and adults, and which is responsive to a changing society.
- To nurture the spiritual, social and moral development of young people by encouraging active consideration of human behaviour and relationships with others.
- To provide for all pupils and students a broad and balanced curriculum which allows them to acquire knowledge, skills, experience and understanding to prepare them for life and work in society as contributors to the common good. To this end, to foster greater understanding and liaison with the world of industry and commerce.
- To ensure continuity of provision at all stages in order to encourage and allow the individual to develop and to experience success.
- To ensure that the education service strives to achieve equality of opportunity for the direct benefit of all those who participate.
- To care for the educational needs of people and the work of the education service, and to foster a love of learning.
- To encourage high standards in all educational behaviour.
- To welcome and encourage the interest and participation of parents, governors, pupils, students and others in all aspects of the educational process.
- To maintain and develop, through high quality training, a workforce of sufficient number and quality to allow the aims of the committee to be supported, recognising particularly the key role of heads of institutions and services.
- To ensure that resources of staff, accommodation, equipment and finance are used flexibly, effectively, efficiently and equitably to meet the aims of the service.

university at a particular cost and level of academic attainment; in a hospital, it may be in terms of the successful throughput of patients. Corporate objectives are usually described in more concrete terms than a mission statement, setting out, for example, the actual target student numbers or a percentage increase in profit. A local education authority may do this in terms of the aspects and areas of education it seeks to support. This may be in the form of a policy statement that provides a guide to specific plans for various parts of the education service, as illustrated in Figure 3.4.

Objectives that fill out the abstractions of the mission statement in more concrete terms are often distinguished from corporate goals or aims, which provide the operational detail that can lead to an action plan. Organisational goals or aims are objectives restated in an operational or measurable form, so that more detail is applied, say, to the size of a change, the timing of it and who is responsible for it. They may be in the form of aspirations, based on particular levels of activity. For example, the goal of a university may be to increase its enrolment by 5% annually over the next five years. This corporate objective has to be defined in terms of how this will be achieved and in which faculties, with identification of resources, marketing and other factors that are necessary to meet the goal.

Activity 3

Does your organisation have clearly defined corporate objectives? If not, write down a list of possible objectives.

3.4 Strategic Planning

Strategic planning is the process of developing and maintaining a viable fit between the organisation's objectives and its resources. It is the next step leading on to a business plan. Corporate strategy is concerned with a wide set of business activities and relationships. In terms of marketing, it is about developing and maintaining a strategic fit between the organisation's goals and resources, and its changing market opportunities.

The strategic marketing plan draws together these strands of organisational planning and direction. The mission, the organisation-wide objectives and the more specific goals serve to indicate the way in which marketing strategies can contribute to corporate strategy.

A marketing programme can assess an organisation's strengths and weaknesses, and evaluate its external objectives in order to achieve greater success for the organisation. The goals set out in the UKCOSA mission statement in Figure 3.5 can form the basis of an action plan for the organisation.

In terms of strategic planning, it can be argued that the military strategy of a country is not an end in itself; it must fit within the overall strategy that determines the country's political goals. In the same way, the marketing strategy identifies the product/service market towards which an organisation plans to commit resources and the foundation on which the organisation attempts to develop a sustained competitive advantage in line with its corporate objectives. This investment in time, money and resources cannot be easily transferred to other product/service markets once the investment has been made. It is for this reason that strategic plans must be considered very carefully.

3.5 **The Customer-orientated Organisation**

In a marketing (customer)-orientated organisation, all marketing

---

Fig 3.5   *UKCOSA mission statement*

The United Kingdom Council for Overseas Student Affairs has a mission statement which states that:

1. UKCOSA is committed to promoting the interests of overseas students studying in the UK. Through this work it tries to further the aims of international education.
2. Primarily, the organisation seeks to promote a comprehensive and coherent policy, consistent and caring practice in the recruitment, reception, education and overall well-being of overseas students.

Its goals are:

1. The provision of support and membership services to member organisations and individual overseas students.
2. The provision of training and consultancy services to members and specifically educational institutions.
3. The organisation and facilitation of research and the provision of information in the field of overseas student affairs.
4. Acting as an advocate in the field of overseas student affairs to governments, international bodies and others.
5. Maintaining the profile of overseas student affairs in government, industrial, commercial and educational planning.
6. Ensuring continuing good practice towards overseas students by government, relevant organisations and educational institutions.

analysis and planning begins and ends with the customer. The marketing objectives are concerned with meeting customers' needs and wants. The organisation will adapt its product/service to the customer and not simply attempt to adapt the customer to fit what the organisation is offering. The organisation's offerings are not seen as inherently desirable, but are adapted to meet the needs of the customers. If a service is not meeting these needs very well, improving the quality and increasing the level of the publicity will not help, and may be based on the erroneous assumption that the consumer is ignorant of what the organisation is offering and its advantages.

Activity 4

Braintree District Council has developed five 'core values'. These are:

1. We are services/customer orientated.
2. We believe in the abilities of the individual.
3. We must be responsive and responsible.
4. We believe in quality.
5. We are action orientated.

(From Local Government Management Board.) Could you apply these values to your own organisation?

In fact, the organisation may not fully understand the needs of the consumer and although it could provide exactly what is needed it does not do this because of its lack of information. A customer-orientated organisation asks:

- To whom are we planning to market?
- Where are they and what are they like?
- What are their current perceptions, needs and wants?
- Will their needs and wants be different in the future when our strategy is implemented?
- How satisfied are our customers with our offerings?

This approach implies a willingness to do more than just consider the offering in different terms, but actually to change the offering within the professional standards and resource constraints that exist.

An entire organisation has to be customer orientated, otherwise one part of it may pull in a different direction. If any part of an organisation is unresponsive to the needs of consumers, they will soon realise that the customer-orientated approach is only a gloss on the surface of an otherwise unresponsive organisation.

Activity 5

How does your organisation deal with suggestions and complaints from customers?

An unresponsive organisation is characterised by a bureaucratic mentality that replaces personal judgement with impersonal policies. The organisation is seen to exist for the needs of the hierarchy rather than for the customer: people's problems are defined in terms of rules rather than personal responses. Non-profit organisations can be particularly prone to this mentality, with unyielding car park attendants and unhelpful receptionists. The out-patient department of a hospital is another case in point, where patients are often organised for the convenience of the consultants rather than the other way around. It can be argued of course that it would be far too expensive to meet every need of the patient; however, it is possible to initiate measures that move in the direction of patient needs without increasing costs. For example, waiting areas can be made more attractive, communication can be improved, waiting time can be reduced and patients can be made to feel welcome.

Activity 6

The London Borough of Hillingdon has developed 'the council's vision'. Their mission is 'to deliver quality service at a price which Hillingdon's residents are prepared to pay'. Do you believe that a 'vision' such as this can lead to action? In their aims, they state that 'we are committed to:

- a continual search for improving quality in everything we do;
- reliable and consistent services which are responsive to needs and delivered to agreed and known standards;
- delivering services to high professional and ethical standards;
- clear and effective communication both with residents and within our own organisation;
- a recognition that people are our most valuable asset;
- the resources of the council being accessible as close as possible to the needs being met;
- becoming a council whose enabling and facilitating style is recognised as a national example of good practice.'

Professionals such as lawyers, accountants and architects may be reluctant to market their services because once the service is marketed it becomes subject to scrutiny. For the same reason, public providers in education, health and social services have been reluctant to market their services. Nevertheless, potential customers require guidance about the quality of a service, its cost to them, and what they will gain from it. They need criteria on which to base judgements about whether to use a service, or which parts of a service they should use. These processes, which offer consumers some measure of determination, are sometimes seen to reduce the control and authority of professional staff.

Unresponsive organisations do not encourage enquiries, complaints, suggestions or opinions from customers. They do not measure customer satisfaction or needs and do not train staff to be customer orientated. The fear is that once the position of the consumers becomes paramount ('consumer sovereignty'), they will start to ask questions about the service being received. A responsive organisation will both welcome and respond to these questions. If parents, for example, are able to choose which school their children will attend, this may increase the incentive of schools to market themselves and to become pupil and parent orientated.

The casually responsive organisation encourages customers to submit enquiries, complaints, suggestions and opinions, and may make periodic studies of consumer satisfaction. However, there may be little follow-up to suggestions, a limited response to enquiries and a lack of a systematic approach to customers. Universities and colleges typically encourage enquiries and suggestions from potential and present students, but are not necessarily well organised to provide more than a limited follow-up. Just as a commercial firm may become more responsive because of changes in its market, so universities and colleges may become more responsive as there is a reduction in the number of school-leavers.

The fully responsive organisation not only surveys current customer satisfaction, but also researches exact customer needs and preferences to discover ways to improve its service. It selects and trains its staff to be customer orientated.

Activity 7

Do you think there is a useful distinction between a mission statement, corporate objectives, marketing objectives and an action plan? How far do these distinctions apply in your organisation?

Colleges that are responsive will understand that students are the most important people on the campus because without them there would be no need for the institution. The students are not dependent on the college, the college is dependent on them, and in that sense the students are doing the college staff a favour by giving them an opportunity to serve them.

In the same way, a responsive school will want to attract as many pupils as possible so that, as a result, it can provide additional activities and a better quality of school life, while also avoiding the possibility of even a small percentage reduction in funding.

In order to improve its image, a school has to offer parents and pupils what it perceives they most want from the school: the parents and pupils are consumers of what the school provides. An approach in which professional staff determine what is appropriate based upon their experience has to be informed by consumer preference.

It can be argued that marketing is a means to an end and is not a substitute for organisational management. The introduction of a customer-orientated philosophy needs to recognise this and should coincide with the organisational planning, so that the marketing plan fits in with the mission statement and the corporate objectives. An organisation will not be able to pursue all its objectives simultaneously; it will have to prioritise them because of a limited budget and because some objectives may be incompatible with each other. For example, a school may want to improve its reputation, improve its classroom teaching, increase pupil numbers, recruit pupils with higher attainment levels, increase the efficiency with which it uses resources, improve the school buildings and so on. The school management will need to concentrate on some objectives in favour of others, based on its perception of the major problems the institution should redress and the budgets available to deal with them.

Activity 8

'Instead of being finance led they ... the health authority ... must go back to first principles and start thinking about what the customer wants – what service do we need to provide for the people of Shropshire, how are we going to do it within our budget and what will our priorities be? ... approaching the problem from the needs of the customer frees management to think more positively, more imaginatively. It was this approach which made it possible for Brighton District Health Authority to launch its cataract fortnight in 1988. By setting up the kind of cataract operation conveyor belt more commonly seen in the Third World, they cleared their waiting list for this simple, but life enhancing operation in just two weeks' (John Harvey-Jones). Can you think of an imaginative approach to problems in your organisation?

3.6 Corporate Planning and the Marketing Plan

Most public sector and non-profit organisations are in a 'high contact' service where the quality of the service is inseparable from the quality of the service provided. In health care, education, police work and so on, human performance naturally shapes the service outcome and hence becomes part of the product. A service involves people dealing with people and the product is relatively intangible – it is produced and consumed simultaneously, and it is often much less standardised than is the case with goods.

In this context, it is particularly important that the marketing plan fits in with what the organisation as a whole wishes to do. This requires a continued interaction between marketing planning and organisational planning. A strategic marketing plan is developed by:

- determining organisation-wide objectives to which marketing strategies must contribute;
- assessing external environmental (in the sense of political, social and economic) threats and opportunities that can be addressed by marketing, in the interest of achieving greater organisational success;
- evaluating present and potential organisation resources and skills in order to take advantage of the opportunities to meet the threats identified in the external environmental analysis;
- deciding on the marketing objectives and specific goals for a relevant planning period;
- formulating the core marketing strategy to achieve specified goals;
- establishing the necessary organisational structure and systems within the marketing function to ensure the implementation of the strategy;
- creating a detailed timetable to carry out the core strategy for the planning period, including a programme of activities and the assignment of specific responsibilities;
- setting up benchmarks to measure interim and final achievement of the programme;
- implementing the planned programme;
- measuring performance and adjusting the core strategy and tactical details as necessary.

The Metropolitan Police action plan in Figure 3.6 states the specific goals of the Force, which can then be put into action. For example, a system of inspection and monitoring can be introduced in order to ensure that 'buildings, vehicles and dress promote pride and confidence in the organisation'.

The Metropolitan Police has developed a programme of action which concentrates on some key areas in which it can achieve a position:

- Where the Force is and feels united and everyone understands and acts upon the common purpose.
- Where the whole energy of the Force is directed at establishing a quality service to the public through a clear process for policy making, and through good leadership and teamwork among and between officers and civil staff.
- Where officers and civil staff working in direct contact with the public are seen to be highly valued; where there is a fair distribution of talent and experience throughout the organisation; and where there is pride in belonging to a team, especially among those providing the 24-hour service.
- Where there is an accepted Metropolitan Police style of policing which can be adjusted to local conditions, making the best use of the people and time available.
- Where all officers and civil staff are and believe they are treated as competent professionals, and where as much attention is given to acknowledging good work as to dealing with shortcomings.
- Where there is a widely understood Metropolitan Police way of communicating by word of mouth and on paper; where internal and external communication is effective, consistent and professional, and unfounded criticism is seen to be challenged promptly and robustly.
- Where paperwork is simplified and produced to a high standard, allowing more time to serve the public.
- Where our buildings, vehicles and dress promote pride and confidence in the organisation among officers, civil staff and the public alike.
- Where there is a valid, reliable range of indicators of performance which measure our achievement, how we operate and how the public view us.

The Force has the goal of continuing to address the need to improve quality of service by:

(a) The reduction of criminal opportunity through crime prevention, public contact and co-operation.
(b) (i) The enhanced detection of specific criminal offences, e.g. robbery, burglary, drug misuse, racial attacks, sexual offences against women and vandalism in accordance with locally and centrally identified principles.
    (ii) An enhanced support, care and concern for victims of crime including the victims of domestic violence.
(c) Improved effectiveness both in the preservation of public tranquillity through closer community/police relations and in the policing of public disorder through tactical control, communications, equipment and training.

Fig 3.6   *The Metropolitan Police action plan*

The 'strategy' describes the 'direction' that the organisation will pursue within its chosen area of work and guides the allocation of resources. Marketing strategy is the marketing logic by which a business expects to achieve its marketing objectives. These objectives are decided by reference to the corporate objectives and are translated into a strategy by analysing market opportunities, and researching and selecting target markets. This process involves making decisions about the organisation's marketing expenditure and the marketing mix of variables available to the organisation.

The marketing plan in a non-profit organisation consists of deciding:

- What business we are in?
- Where do we want to go?

  ⇒   *Mission statement*

- How do we get there?

  ⇒   *Corporate objectives, goals and aims*

- Who are our customers?
- What benefits are they seeking?

  ⇒   *Marketing research*

- What is the context in which we work?

  ⇒   *Audit of external environment – opportunities and threats*

- What do we have to work with?

  ⇒   *Analysis of resources – strengths and weaknesses*

- How do we get there in marketing terms?

  ⇒   *Marketing objectives, goals and aims*

- How do we match objectives and goals with resources and market opportunities?

  ⇒   *Strategic marketing planning*

- When are we going to achieve our objectives and goals?
- Who is responsible for making sure this happens?

  ⇒   *Action plan*

- How well is the strategic marketing plan meeting its objectives?
- What shall we change in our marketing plan?

  ⇒   *Monitoring and review*

The analysis of market opportunities in the process of strategic marketing planning is an essential element of marketing and removes the guesswork from decision making. Marketing has often been described as 'selling goods that don't come back to customers who do', which emphasises the importance of understanding who the customers are and what benefits they are seeking. This is achieved by marketing research.

Activity 9

Braintree District Council developed the title 'Braintree means business' for its management strategy. The scope was broad:

- The concept had to be something for all employees to relate to as well as for customers to relate to.
- It had to cover all the council's activities/services.
- It had to affect the attitudes of all staff towards service, quality and customers.

The aims were equally ambitious:

- To improve the image of the council internally and externally.
- To improve the management style and delivery of services with an emphasis on quality and action.
- To achieve a positive new relationship with customers.

The steps being taken include promotional campaigns, using the logo, leaflets and brochures, and image building. Perhaps even more importantly, the council is also instituting team decentralisation, internal and external surveys, change in recruitment policies, revision of the complaints procedure, and many more initiatives. (From Local Government Management Board.) Are there any initial steps that could be taken to improve the image of your organisation?

3.7 Case Study

A hospital's mission will be to provide good health care to its patients. The change a hospital seeks to make is to turn an ill or injured person into a well person. The objective will be to provide medical services to the best quality in the most cost-effective way, and thereby achieve its mission.

A hospital can emphasise its provision of good health care, the facilities available or its cost effectiveness in its mission statement, and these may reflect the way it works. A concentration on excellent equipment in the hospital may mean a more limited emphasis on patient care, so that good health is achieved by the best facilities rather than the best medical attention and nursing.

The corporate objectives provide more detail and can clarify differences of approach. They may include a statement such as 'to maintain and develop a quality medical facility and to meet the needs of patients in a context which is caring and conducive to good health'. This includes comment on the facilities and the culture of the hospital, which can be spelt out in more detail in further objectives.

A hospital can be orientated towards its patients, foster the abilities of its staff, be responsive to changing needs or concentrate on quality.

If there are suggestions or complaints from patients, the hospital can match them against its mission and objectives. If there is a genuine problem, appropriate action can be taken. For example, if a patient's complaint about the food served in the hospital being inadequate or inappropriate is discovered to be genuine, then it can be improved. This fits in with the mission and objectives of a high quality and caring service.

The hospital's mission can lead to positive action if it has the inclination to see it through. 'Clear and effective communication' can mean improved signposting around the hospital, new reception facilities or an effective appointment system for out-patients. 'A recognition that people are our most valuable asset' can lead to training for nurses and other hospital staff, personnel advice and promotion planning.

The mission statement of the hospital, along with its general objectives and marketing objectives, need to be realistic so that they can be put into action. They have to be operational, otherwise they are only statements of good intention. Put the other way around, a hospital cannot develop an action plan unless it knows in which direction it is going. The hospital needs to make sure that its actions reflect its objectives and mission statement. If high quality is an objective, then this should apply to the way in which patients are cared for, as far as resources allow, and to the fact that suggestions or complaints are dealt with quickly and sympathetically.

A hospital can be dominated by problems of limited resources and as a result can forget that the important principle is the care of patients. However, the patients' needs might be able to be met without spending more money, by using different methods of organising the facilities, for example. A cheerful reception area, an efficient appointment system and clear direction signs are inexpensive ways of improving the quality of the service for patients.

A hospital's image can be improved immediately by giving consideration to car parking for patients and visitors, revising instruction leaflets for patients, carrying out surveys of staff and patients, improving recruitment policies and revising complaint procedures.

4 Marketing Research

4.1 What Is Marketing Research?

[handwritten annotations: Isn't it about your product? or market as it relates to your customers]

Marketing research is the planned, systematic collection, collation and analysis of data designed to help the management of an organisation to reach decisions about its operation and to monitor the results of these decisions. Although the terms 'marketing research' and 'market research' are often used synonymously, market research is in fact concerned with the measurement and analysis of markets rather than the marketing process in these markets. The Market Research Society suggests that 'market(ing) research provides information on people's preferences, attitudes, likes and needs to help companies understand what consumers want'.

[handwritten annotation: Crap]

Marketing research is concerned with the process of marketing within a market and seeks to provide answers to five basic questions: Who? What? When? Where? and How? and perhaps also Why? An organisation wants to know:

- *Who* wants and buys our products/services?
- *What* products/services do people want and what benefits are they looking for?
- *When* will people buy these products/services?
- *Where* will they buy them?
- *How* will they pay?
- *Why* will people buy these products/services and not those of competitors?

The answers to these questions enable a manager to apply an analytical approach to decision making. National and local government, for example, rely on marketing research to provide the data that guides the formulation of policies on a wide range of areas, such as the planning of local transport, the provision of social services and the development of the educational system.

Activity 1

'Councillors and officers may truly believe that they know what the public wants and needs, but in fact, these beliefs are often assumptions based on limited evidence. Providing a better service for the public involves making an effort to test these assumptions, to find out what the public really thinks and feels.

An officer may say, for example, "X way of doing things is good professional practice". Or a councillor may say, "The authority has to act in the public interest". But professional practice can too easily become an end pursued without change in a world where society and public attitudes are changing. Policies can be pursued in the public interest, without any actual test of that interest.' (From Local Government Management Board.) What methods are used in your organisation to test assumptions about the 'public interest'?

Marketing research can reduce uncertainties involved in the decision-making process about marketing activities in general and about specific aspects of marketing, and can help to monitor and control the performance of marketing activities. Information relevant to marketing is collected, recorded, analysed, interpreted and reported about both existing markets and potential markets.

Activity 2

What do you understand by marketing research? List the marketing research activities that are carried out in your organisation. Is there anybody responsible for marketing research?

Non-profit organisations often carry out much less marketing research than those in the commercial sector for several reasons: they have often entered into marketing fairly recently, they have limited budgets and they have limited research experience. In some cases, marketing research is only considered necessary for major decisions, involving large amounts of money, while the use of marketing research should in fact depend on a cost–benefit analysis – the costs of research against the benefits received from it. The costs include the expenses of the research and the costs of delaying a decision while the research is being carried out. The benefits are the improvements made in the decision as a result of the research. If the research can be carried out inexpensively and quickly, it may be worthwhile even for inexpensive decisions. Any reliable information that improves marketing decisions can be considered to be marketing research.

4.2 Marketing Research for Services

As many non-profit organisations provide services, they face the same problems as service industries in carrying out research. Services are intangible and therefore standardisation is difficult. It is difficult to develop accurate descriptions about a service because judgements about a service are influenced by who performs it and the customers' involvement in its performance. Pupils and students can play a large part in the delivery of education and training – they are participants in the process. There is no clear line of demarcation between a service, the place in which it is delivered, the process by which it is delivered and the people involved.

Services have to use relatively 'soft' (qualitative) data rather than 'hard' (quantitative) data in monitoring delivery. The value of a service is in terms of its benefits rather than its features: it depends on the interaction between customers and employers. For this reason, a process known as 'concept testing' can be used to provide a framework to discover whether a potential customer understands the idea of the proposed service, reacts favourably to it and feels it offers benefits that meet unmet needs (Figure 4.1). This depends on whether or not the concept or attributes of the service match the needs of the consumer.

Some services are consumed as they are produced, so that the person or institution providing the service can make appropriate adjustments where these are required by the customers. This is equally true of an airline service as for a hospital or a college. A student at a college of further education is consuming the education and training service at the same time as it is being produced. The lecturing staff are able to make adjustments to the service where required by students, and in fact this is part of the proactive and reactive process of modern education. Many courses in further education are started on a test marketing basis, after identifying consumer needs and then deciding what is required in the course.

Activity 3

Are test marketing procedures used in your organisation?

4.3 Market Research

Market analysis is undertaken to determine the opportunities existing in a particular market and is concerned with an up-to-date knowledge of that market; it is about defining the market, describing it and analysing it. A market is the set of actual and potential consumers of

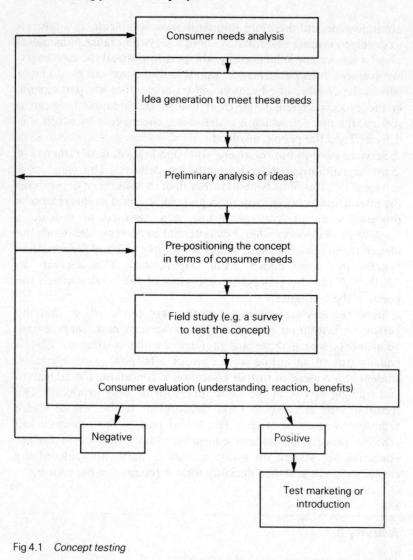

Fig 4.1   *Concept testing*

a market offer in the form of goods and services.

Organisations are likely to be interested in a range of aspects of the market, including:

- the size of the market for a product/service in terms of volume and value;
- the pattern of demand, including the economic, social, political

and technical factors that might influence future demand, and whether it is seasonal or cyclical;

- the market structure in terms of size and number of companies, income groups, sex and age distribution, and geographic location;
- the buying habits of people (both individuals as well as groups such as retailers, wholesalers, and professional and industrial sectors) in the market, including their motivation and procedures;
- the market share of the organisation and how this compares with other periods of time;
- past and future trends in such areas as population, national income and more detailed aspects of an organisation's work;
- overseas markets that may present immediate or long-term opportunities.

For example, a hospital will need to know the size of its locality, the number, sex and age distribution of the population, and any discernible patterns in health. A school will need to know the number of school children in its catchment area, their economic and social background, and the pattern of their school attendance.

Activity 4

Identify the main market for the products/services of your organisation. How does your organisation maintain a detailed understanding of this matter?

This market information is part of the overall picture that is put together in, and derives from, a marketing research strategy to form a marketing intelligence and information system. Managers need to be able to make predictions and decisions based on accurate information. It can be said that market research information is 'neutral', in the sense that it consists of facts about the market, while marketing research information is concerned with attitudes and opinions that need to be interpreted in order to help managers to make decisions.

4.4 Marketing Research Objectives

The Chartered Institute of Marketing has defined marketing as 'the management process responsible for identifying, anticipating and satisfying customer requirements profitably'. For public sector and non-profit making organisations, the concept of 'profitability' may be translated to 'using resources optimally' or 'giving maximum cus-

tomer satisfaction through the most effective deployment of resources'.

The objective of marketing research is to identify and anticipate
customer requirements and to measure whether customers are satisfied with the products/services offered. This is just as important for
assessing customer satisfaction in the public and non-profit sector, by
making the best use of resources, as in the private sector, in order to
make a profit. Customer needs must be the first priority in any
organisation.

Organisations cannot rely simply on providing a good quality
product/service for them to be successful; they have to meet a real
market in a very precise way where the needs of that market may
change fairly regularly. An objective of marketing research is to
make organisations more responsive to these needs. Marketing
research can help an organisation to be proactive as well as reactive.
An organisation that is reactive may simply respond positively to
people's needs when these become apparent, while if it is proactive
it will anticipate needs and help to identify them.

Activity 5

What arguments would you use to convince your organisation that it should spend
more on marketing research?

Research can be defined as a 'careful search or enquiry or endeavour
to discover new facts by a scientific study of a subject'. Decisions in
organisations, particularly marketing decisions, are about the future;
an important objective of marketing research is to help in this
decision-making process by discovering facts which may be well
established but which are nevertheless new to the organisation.

Marketing research may be:

- *descriptive*: in order to inform managers about the marketing
  environment in which the organisation is working. For example, a
  hospital may want to know about the demography of its locality,
  particularly the age profile of the population.
- *explanatory*: in order to inform managers how the marketing
  environment works. This may show what factors are interrelated,
  or what the causal links are between 'situations in the market'. For
  example, a hospital will know who its patients are from its records.
  It may be thought that the patients' satisfaction with the service
  they received from different sections of the hospital is associated

with the age of the various buildings in which the sections are based. It may be found, however, that it is much less to do with this than with the appointment system and the reception process. The age and state of repair of the buildings might have been coincidental.

- *productive*: in order to inform managers about what might happen in the future. The care of patients in terms of arranging appointments and reception/waiting facilities may be felt to be sufficiently important to extend good practice in one area to all areas of the hospital.

4.5 Decisions

The overall purpose of marketing research is to make decisions based on as much evidence as possible. While decisions can be made on hunch or flair alone and may be successful, for longer term survival and success, an organisation needs to put the facts together first and then apply judgement and flair in order to make a decision.

Marketing research assists managers in identifying product/service market opportunities. It also helps them to gain a better understanding of the marketing processes, so that they can develop a more efficient and effective control of the marketing operations. The work involved in marketing research provides the basis for the marketing strategy, policy planning and formulation, and for decision-making purposes. While the information collected helps to resolve uncertainty and risk, it cannot be precise in all details. What actually takes place in the market is conditioned by many factors and variables, which are notoriously unstable in themselves. All the information collected has to be brought together to support marketing decisions.

Activity 6

Describe the process by which decisions are made in your organisation about marketing and product/service design.

Managers need facts on which to base their judgements, but they also have to make decisions in an environment of change: local and/or central government may alter its policy on schools, hospitals or charities; interest rates may rise; or competitors may alter their products/services. Marketing research needs to be a continuous process so that marketing intelligence is kept up to date.

Dana

The needs of customers in particular must be constantly moni-
tored; this has been described as 'keeping close to the customer'. It is
important to know how satisfied they are with the service provided
and how far it satisfies all their needs (or only part of them) in that
particular area. As an organisation's reputation and image can
change over a period of time, it may be possible for an organisation to
encourage customers and potential customers to modify their behaviour to the organisation's advantage. For example, by building up
a good reputation a school may encourage parents to 'send' their
children across local government boundaries.

Activity 7

Is there any contact in the development of your services with:

- local employers;
- schools;
- trade unions;
- other bodies/institutions?

4.6 Methods Used in Marketing Research

Objectives

Once the problem facing a manager in an organisation has been
clearly defined, it is then possible to determine the type of information required to aid the decision-making process (Figure 4.2). This
can lead to a precise definition of the objective of a research project.
Doctors, for example, may want to know how long they need to
spend with each patient in their surgery. Their objective is to match
the length of time they allow for each patient to the immediate needs
of the patient.

Exploratory Stage

In order to find a solution to the problem of how long to spend with
each patient, doctors may explore a number of possibilities: one is to
measure the length of time spent with patients at present; another is
to find out if anybody else has carried out this type of research. This
constitutes an exploratory stage and can help to decide which
methods of collecting information would be most suitable in any
investigation to be carried out.

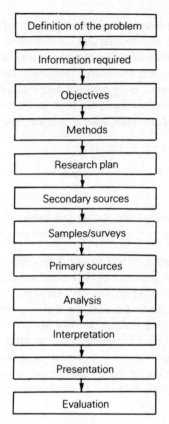

Fig 4.2 *The research process*

Sources of Information

Primary information is data collected by or on behalf of the people who are going to make use of it. If the doctors conduct a 'field' survey, this will produce primary data.

Secondary information is data used by people other than those for whom it was collected. If the doctors use someone else's research, this is secondary or 'second-hand' data. Such data may be just what the doctors are looking for or it may have to be adapted to fit their needs.

Secondary data may be collected for one purpose and used for another. For example, the appointment book may show how many patients were seen by a number of doctors at their surgeries, but may not show how long each patient actually spent with them. Secondary data is often a compromise between what people want and what they are able to find. However, it is cheap to obtain, a variety of data is available and the information may have been collected over a long period of time, so that trends can be identified.

Organisations may find that they have internal sources of data that are useful in a market research process. The internal accounting system, for example, may provide large quantities of information. General marketing intelligence, such as information about the national economy or the local labour market, may be relatively easy to obtain.

Activity 8

Carry out a quick survey of the marketing information available in your organisation.

Statistics published by government departments and/or local authorities tend to be the product of either an 'administrative process' or of specially conducted enquiries or surveys. For example, a local authority may collect statistics on the local labour market, which would be useful to a college setting up a training unit. While this information may be of general use, in that it may indicate skill shortages and employment opportunities, it may be of limited direct use in showing training needs. A special survey would need to be carried out by the training unit to obtain more specific information.

Desk Research

This is usually the first stage in the research process because it is work that can be carried out literally at the marketing researcher's desk. Internal records will be an important element of this research. Statistical details about employees can be obtained through personnel records while aspects of the work of an organisation can be investigated via the purchasing accounts or through consideration of any monitoring system that exists. Visitors' books, consultants' appointment lists, teachers' timetables and accommodation schedules may all play a part.

External sources of information can also be investigated at the researcher's desk, including publications by central government, local authorities, academic researchers, trade associations and commercial organisations. There is also a range of specialist agencies who provide information, such as GALLUP, which is best known for opinion polls, and the Joint Industry Committee for Television Audience Research (JICTAR), which provides statistics on television audiences.

Desk research should throw some light on to the problem under investigation and show what further information is required. A company's internal information system is usually designed to produce a continuous stream of data that can measure current performance and indicate trends. It may establish a base-line for change and suggest a basis for resource allocation. It also provides an early warning system and signals change, as well as indicating areas for further research. This can include updated enrolment figures for a college or patient admissions for a hospital.

Desk research may also include 'modelling'. This is an attempt to understand the reality of a situation through changing the variables in a 'model'. Computer modelling involves programming as many variables as possible and then introducing change to see what happens. For example, if prices are raised for a particular service, the question may be how many consumers will continue to buy the service. Such modelling has been used to investigate the effect of subscription fees for clubs and societies as well as charges for entry into museums.

Activity 9

Investigate the strategies used by a museum in order to promote attendance.

Field Research

Once the sources of desk research have been exhausted, field research may become necessary. This includes all the various survey and sampling methods that can be used to solve the manager's problem(s). Once away from the 'desk', the research process is usually more expensive in both time and resources, and the amount of research that can be carried out is dependent on the money available. The methods available for collecting field data are discussed in Chapter 5.

4.7 The Marketing Research Budget

This is often based on past costs and a historical increment may be applied so that the budget is adjusted upwards or downwards by a percentage that is based on the expected level of activity of the organisation. Some budgets are based on the amounts spent by other similar organisations. In the private sector, the budget may be based on a percentage of expected revenue, while in the public sector it may be what is felt to be affordable, which may mean what is left over when other 'more necessary' activities have been met.

These approaches imply that marketing research is a discretionary activity rather than an essential tool for effective management. A research budget needs to be established in order to achieve targets, whether these are satisfied patients in a hospital or target student numbers in a college or university. Marketing research is often regarded as a luxury that is only worth financing when it can be easily afforded.

However, it can be argued that it is in fact a necessity, which is even more true when there are problems and the market is difficult. It is at these times that it is even more important for an organisation to understand its customers and its market. When there is a demographic downturn, as happened, for example, in the number of school-leavers in the UK between 1985 and 1995, it is even more essential for schools, colleges and universities to understand their pupils and students. It is at these times that marketing research can be of particular help to managers in making difficult decisions, and of course more money needs to be made available for it. In the same way, marketing research can help managers to prioritise activities in organisations that have a wide range of activities and are faced with new initiatives.

In the non-profit sector, it will usually be impossible to measure the effectiveness of marketing research by the extra revenue or profits generated. It is possible, however, to use a cost–benefit analysis. In this approach, the manager costs the research to be carried out in a particular period and then estimates the benefits that are expected to be gained. A college, for example, may cost the expenses of carrying out research into an area of potential student interest and compare this with the number of students it expects to enrol as a result. The equation between costs and benefits involves consideration of alternative decisions and estimating the economic opportunity cost of choosing the wrong course of action. For example, the college might research the possible number of overseas students it could attract; however, setting up an administrative structure to receive these students when it is unlikely to attract any could be an expensive mistake.

Once the desk research has been completed and the resources that are available have been identified, the next stage is to select the appropriate survey and sample method.

4.8 Case Study

A library can ask users about their needs. Questions can include the ease of use of library services, the importance of reference and other sections, the use of the catalogue and advice from staff. How much notice is taken of book borrowers varies, or those of people who use the library only to read the daily newspapers or to view an art exhibition.

Marketing research is the planned, systematic collection, collation and analysis of data that is designed to help the management of an organisation to reach decisions about its operation and to monitor the results of these decisions. The library can investigate who uses its services and the frequency with which these services are used. It can ascertain the benefits that users are seeking, as well as the type and form of library service they want. An assistant librarian may be responsible for the marketing research activities of a library.

The library may try out new ideas to see how well they work. A mobile library service or a service by post may be tried to see if it can be organised cost effectively. Introducing a coffee shop may be 'test marketed' in order to see how successful it is.

The main market for a library may be book borrowing, and this can be encouraged by promotion and publicity. The book borrowing 'habit' can be fostered by having close links with schools and other organisations, and encouraging such events as school visits to the library.

Convincing the local authority that more money should be spent on marketing research will depend on the attitude towards the service. If the objective is to spend as little as possible, marketing research may not be a high priority, while if the emphasis is on the quality of the service, then it will be. As a library service becomes more autonomous and is judged on its services, the need for marketing research will grow. Research information will be invaluable in helping a library to understand its markets, be clear about its image and know what its customers want.

Decisions about the various services provided by a library may be made in the light of external requirements, such as the requirements of the local authority. Decisions will be made by the head librarian and by assistant librarians depending on their delegated authority.

A library needs to have contact with schools and other educational institutions in order to encourage their pupils and students to use library services. Local employers and other organisations may want to make use of information services as well as provide sponsorship.

Marketing information can include the number and type of books borrowed, the list of library card holders, information on local services, educational facilities, career opportunities and so on. Some libraries have specialised data on local history or on the economy of the area.

A museum, or library for that matter, can improve attendance by a better understanding of its potential customers' wants, providing for these wants and telling people about this provision. As well as attractive displays, a gift shop, cafe, coffee shop and other facilities may encourage attendance. The museum can advertise its displays and facilities in the local library.

5 Collecting Marketing Information

5.1 Introduction

Once desk research has exhausted all the available internal or secondary sources of information, the next stage is to collect information especially for the purpose it is required. A local authority will, for example, be able to find out about the use of a service by looking at records, but it may only be possible to measure the satisfaction with a service by carrying out a survey of users.

Activity 1

'The London Borough of Richmond-upon-Thames found through surveys that four out of five people use the telephone to contact the council about refuse collection and street lighting, where only one in three used it to contact them about rent/rate rebates or housing benefits. After the survey, the council introduced a single telephone number for offices in one area, and introduced "direct dialling in" for sections with regular contact with the public.' (From Local Government Management Board.) Does your organisation use the results of surveys to make changes in its systems? If it does, list some examples; if it does not, list reasons for introducing surveys and how results may be applied.

The collection of information may be on a *quantitative* basis through a survey procedure, in order to collect facts and figures, and/or by a *qualitative* process, in order to explore people's views and analyse their concerns. The qualitative process will usually be in the form of an unstructured interview or a group discussion. The decision on the method to use depends on what information is required and how it is to be used. If hard facts are required for a performance review exercise, then a survey may be the best method, while if information on attitudes and perceptions is required, a group discussion might produce the best result. The main methods used for collecting information are:

- desk research – secondary, primary;

- field research – observation, interviewing, questionnaires, sampling.

5.2 **Observation**

A limited enquiry can be carried out quickly by observation. For example, the use made of a reference section of a library may be observed and recorded, or the interest in an item in a museum may be measured by observing the frequency the item is looked at and the length of time people stand in front of it. Closed-circuit television has made it possible to do this unobtrusively.

This form of enquiry is limited, because only a small amount of information is collected. The reason for people's interest or lack of it cannot be discovered this way. Interviews or questionnaires are required to obtain information of this kind.

Activity 2

Use observation to investigate some aspect of your organisation. Consider the usefulness of the results.

Participant observation is used in an attempt to increase the amount of information that can be obtained. For example, an observer can join a class in a school and take part in its activities in order to observe closely the behaviour of the pupils and the teacher. The problems with this approach are that it is very time consuming and the observer's presence may cause the pupils and the teacher to behave abnormally.

Systematic observation is usually more useful in marketing research. This is used to observe events only when the participants will not know that they are being observed. This method can be used to observe the use made of different parts of a service, such as a library or museum as already suggested. If parts of the reference library are observed to be never used whereas other sections are used heavily, this could lead to a redistribution of the service to take into account consumer preferences.

The main problems with observation are:

- *objectivity*: in order to remain objective the observer cannot ask the very questions that will help in an understanding of the event;
- *selectivity*: the observer can be unintentionally selective in choosing what to record;

- *interpretation*: the observer may interpret observed behaviour in ways which the people themselves do not intend;
- *chance*: an isolated action may be assumed to be a recurrent one;
- *realisation*: if people realise that they are being observed, they may change their behaviour.

5.3 Interviewing

In an interview, full use is made of all means of communication. An interview can be described as a *conversation with a purpose*. As with observation in an informal sense, everybody uses this method to obtain information: consumers observe the price of goods in shops and make comparisons; patients observe the quality of service in a hospital. When a patient asks in the out-patient department 'How long will I have to wait?', this may be followed by supplementary questions about why there is a long waiting time, as well as whose fault it is! The purpose of this conversation may be two-fold: to obtain information and to assign responsibility.

A *formal interview* is a conversation between two people that is initiated by the interviewer in order to obtain information. The interviewer will introduce each topic by means of a specific question and will decide when the objective of the interview has been satisfied. In marketing research, interviews are frequently based on a list of prepared questions. In a very formal interview, set questions are asked and the answers noted or ticked off in a series of boxes. In a more informal situation, the questions may follow a pattern but will vary between interviews according to the responses of the person or people being interviewed.

Activity 3

Consider the requirements of a well-organised job selection interview. What are the difficulties that may arise?

Marketing research interviews often take the form of a set series of questions, because the answers can then be readily recorded, collated and analysed, and the research interviewer does not need any particular skills. In surveys about consumer spending habits or use of consumer durables, the same questions may be asked in each survey. In these cases, research interviewers need to have the qualities of conscientiousness and consistency. Where market research is investigating people's attitudes and natures, more skill may be required in follow-up and secondary questions in order to elicit information and retain a high level of objectivity.

Interviewing Skills

Interviewing is one of the most important ways of carrying out research. Public sector and non-profit organisations that want to find out how people feel about their service or why they use the service will employ interviewing to discover people's attitudes and motives. However, interviews are not uniformly successful, but there are skills in interviewing that can be learnt.

In marketing research, these skills can be acquired by training, careful preparation and by experience. Research interviewers will differ in their skills while the people being interviewed, the respondents, will differ in their interest and reaction. Interviewing is a subjective process that relies heavily on good communication. If the people involved do not like each other or have different ideas about the way the interview should be conducted, the objectives are not likely to be fulfilled.

The way in which questions are asked may affect the answers. If the research interviewer asks a question in the form 'You are satisfied with the service you received in this hospital, aren't you?', this indicates a particular answer. If the question is asked in the form 'What are your views on the services you have received in this hospital?', it leaves it much more open for the respondent to express his/her own point of view.

The location at which questions are asked may also be very important. If a research interviewer is stopping people on their way into a hospital, they may want to answer the questions very briefly and quickly, in order not to be late for an appointment; however, if they are approached while waiting inside the hospital, they may be only too happy to have someone with whom to talk.

Interviewer bias may arise from: a subtle influencing of the results by the way questions are asked, the extent of supplementary questions, the sequence of questions or the categorisation of interviewees as related to their age and appearance; and a less subtle influencing of the results by poor recording of the answers or the fabrication of answers in order to avoid the effort involved in collecting them.

The Role of the Respondent

The respondent plays an essential part in the success of an interview. The respondent has to want to answer the questions being asked and has to be able to answer them, in the sense of having the information.

Motivation is an important factor: if the respondent knows why the questions are being asked, then he/she may feel that it is worthwhile answering them; if the respondent feels that he/she can influence events, this may be an important motivation. For example, a service may be improved as a result of the survey. Paying people to respond may provide an incentive but it may also mean that people who know very little about the subject, and are therefore unsuitable for the research purpose, are interviewed.

Respondents also need to know what information is relevant and the expected length of the answer. For example, a respondent may want to talk at length about the problems of travelling to the hospital when the research is concentrating on the service that the hospital provides.

5.4 **Questionnaires**

A questionnaire is a list of questions aimed at discovering particular information. In marketing research, questionnaires are used to carry out many kinds of field work. They can be used in interviews to standardise the questions and they can be used in observation to make it more systematic, by requiring the observers to answer a list of questions about what they are observing. Questionnaires can be distributed by hand and then collected when they are completed. This method of distribution encourages people to answer the questions and ensures return of the forms. However, it is expensive because the people distributing and collecting the questionnaires have to be paid.

Activity 4

Construct a short questionnaire to evaluate the eating facilities available in your organisation and test it on a small number of your colleagues.

Postal questionnaires are cheaper to distribute than those delivered by hand and they can be sent to larger numbers of people. However, there is usually a low response rate unless there is a very strong incentive to return the forms, but this can mean that the response is unrepresentative. Also, it is not possible to explain personally the meaning of the questions, or how to complete the form, except by written instructions.

Good question design is an essential element of any questionnaire. The questions should reflect the aims and objectives of the survey, so that a survey enquiring into the effects of charging for museum entrance should contain questions clearly relevant to that subject. If it has already been decided to charge an entrance fee and the real purpose of the survey is to find out how much people would be prepared to pay, then the questions should be about that.

Questions, therefore, should be:

- *simple and clear*, so that the targeted respondents can easily understand them;
- *relevant*, so that they produce the desired information;
- *in a logical order*, so that they help the respondent to remember the answers;
- *unambiguous*, so that they leave the meaning clear;
- capable of being answered *without embarrassment*.

Hypothetical questions, asking 'What would you do if . . .', are of limited value although they may lead to respondents thinking about their answers and the issues involved. Leading questions, asking 'Don't you think action should be taken . . .', encourage a particular answer (in this case a positive one). Multiple-choice questions can be used to produce a qualitative response.

The questionnaire form needs to be carefully designed if it is going to be completed accurately and fully. The instructions for completion need to be precise so that it is clear who should complete the form. How and where the answers are to be recorded should be obvious with sufficient space for a full answer to be given. Many forms in fact do not provide enough space, even for such obvious and essential pieces of information as the address.

5.5 Sampling

In marketing research, considerable use is made of sampling. *A sample is anything less than a full survey of a population* and it is usually a small part of a population, where the 'population' is the group of people or items about which information is being collected (such as parents of pupils attending a particular school).

Sampling has a statistical basis and it can only be understood in these terms. It can be shown statistically that a reasonably large sample selected at random from a population will, on average, represent the characteristics of the population, subject to a mathematically calculable error. The selection of the sample must:

- be at random, so that every item in the population has an equal chance of being selected;

- include a large enough number of items to represent the whole population;
- be larger the more variable and less homogeneous the population. A larger sample will be necessary if the people being sampled have widely ranging opinions, to be sure that all opinions are included.

The size of a sample is independent of the population size; it is a matter of judgement based on:

- the inclusion of at least a minimum number of items in order to be representative;
- the variability of the population;
- the degree of accuracy required;
- the resources available to pay for the cost of the sample survey.

It is only in limited circumstances that a full survey is carried out. This occurs when the 'population' is small or resources are large. It may be possible to survey all the patients entering a particular ward in a hospital in a week. It is only possible to survey the whole population of the country in the Population Census by carrying it out at ten yearly intervals and putting considerable resources towards it because it is felt to be worthwhile.

In carrying out marketing research on people's opinions about a service or the use of a product, there is usually neither the time nor the money for a survey of all possible users; therefore, samples are widely used.

Samples are:

- cheaper than a survey;
- quicker than a survey;
- often more reliable than a survey – resources can be concentrated on fewer questionnaires and research interviewers to obtain reliable information.

Sample Error
Sample error can arise as a result of problems with the sample design (non-sampling error) and/or problems in the sampling process (sampling error). If there are errors in the design of the sample, this can lead to bias.

Sampling error is the difference between the estimate of a value and the actual value. For example, a sample survey may show that the average age of students entering a college of further education is 16 years 6 months, when in fact it is 16 years 10 months. The sampling error is four months.

Sampling error arises because a sample, even when chosen at random, will not exactly represent the 'population' from which it has been chosen. The degree of a sampling error will depend on the size of the sample, not the size of the population from which it has been chosen. A 'population' of one million does not require a larger sample than a 'population' of 100,000.

The importance of sampling data is that, in a random sample, it is possible to measure the probability of errors of any given size and therefore to increase or decrease the size of the sample to achieve the degree of accuracy required. The sample needs to be sufficiently accurate for the results to be of help in the decision-making process.

Activity 5

Does your organisation use sampling for any purpose? Which of the various sampling methods do you consider to be the most appropriate for your type of organisation?

In fact, errors often arise from the sample design and the way in which the sample survey is carried out.

Sample Design
A sample design will include:

- *the sample unit* – the people or units in the sampling population. If the sample is based on hospital patients, it is important that visitors are not included.
- *the sample frame* – the list of people or units from which the sample is taken. The list of patients of a hospital, for example, needs to be comprehensive and complete.
- *the survey method* – the questionnaires need to be designed and methods of distribution decided. If interviews or observation are to be used, these need to be effectively organised.
- *the sample method* – which has to be chosen.

Sample Methods
There is a range of sample methods from which to choose:

Random samples:
- simple random;
- systematic;
- stratified.

Semi or quasi-random samples:
- random route;
- quota;
- cluster.

Non-random:
- convenience;
- snowball;
- judgement;
- focus group;
- piggybacking;
- omnibus;
- off-the-peg;
- syndicated.

Some of these methods are fully random, while others contain only an element of randomness. The sampling error can be calculated in a random sample, but this is difficult to assess in non-random samples.

Simple Random Samples

Each unit (or person) in the population has an equal chance of being included in a simple random sample. A lottery method 'without replacement' is used for selection, so that once a unit has been selected it cannot be chosen again.

This sampling method is particularly suitable when a population is relatively small and the sampling frame is complete. However, as this is not usually the case in marketing research – populations are large and sampling frames are incomplete – less fully random methods are often used.

Systematic Random Sampling

This is random sampling with a system based on regularity. A name or unit is chosen at random from the sampling frame, and then a name or unit is selected at regular intervals from the randomly chosen point. The extent of the intervals depends on the size of the sample required. For example, if a 2% sample is required from a sampling frame of 10,000 names, then the 200 names required are selected at intervals of 50 starting from the randomly chosen name. If this is 35, the next name selected is the 85th on the sampling frame, the next the 135th and so on.

This method is often used in marketing research because it facilitates the selection of sampling units particularly where sampling frames such as the electoral register or a housing list are used.

However, researchers need to be aware of the fact that the use of systematic selection can lead, by chance, to bias. For example, if houses are built on a regular plan, it is possible that every sampling unit selected will be a detached house while the list in fact includes many semi-detached and terraced houses. Consequently, the sample may be unrepresentative of the population from which it is drawn.

Stratified Random Sampling

This method makes a virtue of the main problem of systematic sampling by dividing the sampling frame into groups or categories. Each person or unit can only be in one group or 'stratum'. A simple random sample or systematic sample is selected within each stratum: if the same proportion of each stratum is taken, then the overall result will be representative of the whole population. For example, if the list of houses can be divided into three groups, say detached, semi-detached and terraced, then the households can be selected in proportion to the number of houses in each group.

Random Route Sampling

This is a form of systematic sampling used in marketing research surveys. The sampling frame is usually a list of properties such as houses, shops, factories and offices. An address is selected at random as a starting point and the researcher is then given instructions to identify further addresses by taking alternate left-hand and right-hand turns at road junctions and calling at every sixth address (whatever it happens to be: house, shop, office) '*en route*'.

In marketing research on consumer durables, for example, it is possible to choose an estate or a suburb that has the correct socio-economic characteristics for the consumers being targeted. The process of carrying out the research is straightforward. It is, however, a semi or semi-quasi random method because the element of selection can be strong. It can be used to follow up the results of test marketing or to gather opinions quickly. A hospital can use this method to find out what image it has with, say, council house tenants or middle-class house owners.

Quota Sampling

Again, this is heavily used in marketing research because it is possible to 'target' precisely a group of consumers. The quotas are chosen so that the overall sample will accurately reflect known population characteristics in a number of respects. It is not random because every individual does not have the same probability of being included in the sample.

Public sector organisations may want to know the opinions of people in certain age groups and in particular income brackets, on the basis of age and probable income. Research interviewers will have a quota of people in each age/income group to fill. Early questions may check on the respondent's characteristics by asking age and income level. The distribution may be by selecting people waiting in a hospital out-patient department, or at enrolment sessions at a college.

The greater the number of population characteristics that are introduced, the more difficult it is for research interviewers to select the respondent. It may not be too difficult to find people aged between 30 and 40 years who earn close to the national average salary, but add characteristics such as sex, educational level, and so on, and the task becomes impossible. Nevertheless, it is a quick and cheap way to carry out marketing research where the required characteristics are limited.

Cluster Sampling
This is used in marketing research usually as a geographical or 'area' method. For example, a region or a town may be broken down into smaller areas. A few of these areas are then selected by random methods and individual or whole households within these areas are selected again by random methods to form the clusters to be sampled.

The sampling frame is usually a map, and once an area has been selected, systematic or random route sampling may be used. Research can be carried out quickly by sending a team of researchers to cover one cluster after another.

This method can provide a quick response to questions – for example, about the use that people make of the local library service. Although there are elements of randomness in it, it is not a method in which every individual in an area has an equal chance of selection. Also, the smaller areas selected may have similar characteristics, which does not make them representative. It is, therefore, a method of sampling with only some elements of randomness, adding to the information available to an organisation about its marketing but not providing a high level of reliability.

Multi-stage Sampling
There is a range of ways of organising research samples that have been found to be useful in particular circumstances. In multi-stage sampling, a series of samples are taken at successive stages. In multi-phase sampling, some information is collected from the whole sample while additional information is collected from subsamples of the whole sample. Repeated or inter-penetrating sampling involves

selecting a number of subsamples, rather than one full sample, from a population. A master sample is one that covers the whole country to form the basis for smaller local samples.

These methods are used to sample very large populations, such as the whole population of a country. Opinion polls apply these methods in order to arrive at a relatively small sample (say 2000 voters) that is still representative of the regions as well as the views of electors. Public sector organisations may use these methods when they have a large number of employees, perhaps in different units in various geographical locations.

Activity 6

List the biases that could occur if a museum decided to interview every tenth person entering the museum next Friday morning between 10.00 and 12.00 a.m. Suggest how you could reduce or eliminate these biases.

Non-random Methods

Simple random sampling, systematic sampling and stratified sampling have a sufficiently random element in them to enable the assessment of sampling errors. Other methods usually attempt to include some element of randomness in order to achieve the same result. Providing there is strict control over the sample design, implementation and interpretation, all these methods can produce reliable results. There are also 'quick and dirty' methods that can be used by an organisation to obtain extra information on an issue quickly:

- *Convenience sampling* consists of soliciting information from any convenient group whose views may be relevant to the subject of the enquiry. For example, hospital patients may be asked their views on a new appointment system, or a student group in a college may be asked its views on the enrolment procedure.
- *Snowball sampling* involves asking participants in convenience sampling to suggest the names of other people like them who could be contacted and interviewed. This could add a group without the same bias as the original one; for example, potential hospital patients or friends of the students who have not yet enrolled for the college.
- In *judgement sampling*, respondents are selected on the basis of

the researcher's opinion that they constitute a representative cross-section of the population to be investigated. They have not, of course, been chosen at random.

- In *focus group interviewing*, the researcher interviews small groups of consumers that have been targeted to provide a clear focus on particular matters. They could be, for example, new full-time students in a particular age group being asked about their views on entry procedures to a college.

- *Piggybacking* involves adding questions to an existing survey or using an established form of distribution to conduct a survey. For example, an evaluation questionnaire may be distributed with the enrolment form of a college, to check on how easy it has been to find out about courses and to complete the enrolment procedures. This can also be called 'omnibus' research, in the sense that other organisations can climb aboard an existing survey.

- In particular circumstances, it may be possible to obtain information from specialist research organisations. They can provide *made-to-measure* surveys and samples, as well as *off-the-peg* research, which is data they have generated. In the latter case, either the data or the system for collecting it can be bought 'off-the-peg'. They may also produce *syndicated* research, which is data that is of value to a number of organisations but which would be too expensive for any of them to collect individually.

Panels

In marketing research, considerable use is made of panels. These are samples in the sense that groups of people are selected from the survey population by a random process. The groups form a panel of people who are questioned for information at various intervals over a period of time. This means that the same questions are asked to the same group of people at different instances over a period of time.

Researchers use this method to judge such matters as the success of a promotion campaign, changes in views about the image of an institution, and changes in the behaviour patterns of the people on the panel. The main problem with this method is that the people on the panel may become atypical of the population they 'represent'. This 'panel conditioning' arises because panels become alerted to the subjects of the questions they are asked and may begin to notice changes to a greater extent than they would if they were not members of the panel. In the same way, they may alter their own behaviour because they know they will be questioned about it.

The use of panels enables market researchers to rate changes over a period of time, whereas most sample methods provide a 'snapshot' of the situation at a particular time. A charity introducing a new promotional campaign to raise funds may use panels to judge whether its image has been changed in the desired way by the campaign.

5.6 **Experiments**

Experiments are used in marketing research to measure the effect of changes in one variable or another. Two groups of people can be 'matched', for example, for factors such as age and income level which might affect their attitudes. The two groups need to be chosen randomly so that the differences between them can be measured.

In the 'before–after' experimental design, an 'experimental group' is exposed to, say, a new promotion campaign, while a 'control' group is not. In this way, attitudes and changes in attitudes can be compared between the two groups. If the results show a 'positive' change in attitude in the experimental group, the campaign may be judged to have been successful.

Experiments are used where the results need to be accurate and the area of study is narrow, so that the variables involved can be controlled. This is easier in physical sciences such as chemistry and biology than it is in marketing. However, these methods may be used successfully in test marketing; for example, when a charity wants help in deciding on a new logo or advertisement, experimental methods can be applied.

Activity 7

Design an experiment that would 'prove' that a specific mail shot was effective.

5.7 **Conclusion**

The objective of marketing research is to discover customers' requirements and to measure how far these are being met by the services/products currently available. For example, a hospital can investigate the level of satisfaction that patients have with present services and what other services they would like; colleges and universities can ascertain the needs of potential students, as well as evaluating students' satisfaction with the courses they are on; charities can research the factors determining the decisions of donors to contribute to their funds and how donors would like these funds spent.

Activity 8

In Cheshire County Council, extensive work has been undertaken by the Libraries and Museums Service on measuring the degree of satisfaction experienced by users and perceived by non-users in an area of the county where a new town and a new public library have recently been established.

An initial survey, conducted in 1977, set out to determine the needs of potential users of a new district library to ascertain the size of the latest demand for library services, the characteristics of the proposed users, what facilities would be required, which location would maximise use, how the library should operate when opened and what effect it would have on existing libraries in the area. Data was gathered from:

- a survey of residents in the community;
- a survey of current users of both the old library and mobile;
- a survey of organisations in the area;
- discussions with select groups of potential users (and non-users).

The 1984 follow-up survey revealed the value of such detailed planning and provision . . . . The results were very encouraging . . . the usage of library facilities had more than doubled since 1977 . . . attitudes amongst users were very positive . . . towards the services provided and the books available. (From Yorke, D., Local Government Management Board.) In the light of this example, consider the marketing research methods that would be appropriate for your organisation.

Most organisations will have target markets on which they will concentrate, once these are identified. A college of further education may consider that its main target market (primary market) is the 16–19 age group. It will also have subsidiary or secondary markets, such as adults or employers with training needs. The organisation will bring both of these markets into sharp focus by marketing research to identify the particular benefits they are seeking.

5.8 Case Study

A secondary school might carry out a survey of sixth formers to discover what facilities they would like to have in a proposed new sixth form centre. Parents might be surveyed to discover their views on trips abroad: which countries to visit, for how long, the best time of year, how much they would be prepared to pay.

Observation of the use of the school library might show that it is used for a variety of purposes: for research and as a study project room, as a social centre and meeting place. This could lead to a reorganisation of the library, to meet some of these different needs better, and to meet others, such as a social centre, in other ways.

The headteacher will have prepared well for an interview for a member of staff by producing a job description and person specification, a list of questions and a summary of short-listed candidates. The interview panel will also have been well prepared. In addition, the candidates will have been briefed by being shown around the school, and given the opportunity to ask questions and find out about the job. The interview will be carried out in comfortable surroundings and free from interruption. Each candidate will be asked similar questions. These preparations and this type of interview format can limit any problems that might arise as a result of misunderstandings about the 'role' of the candidates and from interviewer bias.

A school might construct a short questionnaire on its dining hall to be distributed to all the pupils, but first tried out on members of staff:

1. Where do you normally eat lunch?
    (a) in the dining hall
    (b) in a classroom
    (c) elsewhere

2. If you use the dining hall, how would you rate **A.** the choice and **B.** the quality of the food? (Ring as appropriate.)

    A. (i) Good   **B.** (i) Good
           (ii) Satisfactory   (ii) Satisfactory
           (iii) Poor   (iii) Poor

3. If you have ticked satisfactory or poor to either **A.** or **B.** in question 2, what improvements would you like to see?

Instead of distributing this questionnaire to the whole school, it could be distributed to a sample of pupils. This could be a simple random sample, say 10% of the pupils. Or it could be stratified by age or by class and then 10% distributed to each stratum. Both methods would have the advantage of including a strong random element.

If a sample was chosen by distributing questionnaires to pupils entering the dining hall between 12.00 a.m. and 1.00 p.m. on a Friday, the results may be biased by chance factors: if it is raining, for example, more pupils may use the dining hall than usual; some pupils may only use the dining hall on a Friday, while some pupils may never use it on a Friday. In these circumstances, the results could not be applied across the week. However, a survey taken each lunch hour throughout a week would help to reduce these biases, particularly if the questionnaire asked about the usual use made of the dining hall.

In an attempt to try to discover how to encourage healthy eating, a secondary school might carry out the following experiment. The lunch-time eating habits of two classes in the same age group are observed. One class is then given science lessons on the benefits of a balanced diet while the other class is not. The eating habits of the two classes are then observed to see if there have been any discernible changes.

A school can use all the various types of marketing research as far as resources are concerned. For example, to measure satisfaction with the school, interviews can be carried out with parents and pupils, questionnaires can be distributed to a sample of parents, and school-leavers can be given exit interviews.

6 The Marketing Audit

6.1 What Is a Marketing Audit?

Non-profit organisations need to know their current position in relation to their market(s), as well as the social, political and economic environment in which they are working. They do this through a marketing audit, which is a formal review of everything that has affected or may affect the organisation's marketing environment, internal marketing system and specific marketing activities. Such a review will include an analysis of the way the organisation carries out marketing research, its marketing organisation and strategies, and its marketing objectives. It will consider the organisation's marketing in terms of products/services, prices, place and promotion (the four 'Ps'). It will study the organisation's markets, customers and competitors, and the overall economic, political, cultural and technical environment.

An organisation's marketing environment consists of all the factors that are external to its own marketing system and that impinge on a successful exchange process with its customers. These factors can be collected into categories, sometimes referred to as the STEP factors:

- *s*ocial factors;
- *t*echnological factors;
- *e*conomic factors;
- *p*olitical factors.

Activity 1

Which of the STEP factors have the greatest impact on your organisation and its marketing activities?

6.2 Social Factors

Non-profit organisations need to take account of social factors that affect their activities. These social factors include population, education, and environmental and cultural aspects of an organisation's work.

Demography

People make up markets so that population trends are an essential part of an organisation's environment. Changes in age structure are an important consideration for most organisations. Schools, colleges and universities, for example, need to know about the birth rate because most of their pupils and students are in particular age groups, so changes in the birth rate will affect their potential market in the years to come. For example, the post Second World War baby boom was matched by an expansion in educational establishments in the 1950s and 1960s. But the lower birth rate that followed in the 1960s and 1970s meant that a painful reappraisal had to be made, particularly in the number of school places required. Further and higher education institutions have been able to combat the fall in numbers in the post-school age groups to some extent by enrolling mature students and by extending their activities into new markets, such as training for industry. However, schools do not have the same flexibility and many education authorities have had to close schools as a result of the reduction in the level of demand for school places.

Changes in life expectancy are of particular interest to public sector organisations such as hospitals. The increase in the number of old people may be matched to some extent by a general improvement in people's health; nevertheless, it does put greater pressure on the health service and creates a need for a greater number of hospital beds. This trend has also led to a greater need for old people's homes, but since the public sector has had difficulty in meeting this need, it has encouraged the development of a private sector growth industry.

Geographical shifts in population arise as people move into towns and cities from rural areas, from city centres to the suburbs, and from the north and west to the southeast. People move to find work or because they have obtained a job in a different area, because of retirement, to improve their housing standard and so on. These shifts in population create changes, particularly over a period of time, for many public sector institutions. Schools may find that the number of their pupils rises or falls; hospitals may find their services in greater or lesser demand; sports and leisure facilities, libraries, social service facilities and so on will also feel the same effects.

Activity 2

What influence do the following have on the work of your organisation?

- demographic trends;
- changes in leisure habits;
- attitudes towards education and training;
- levels of unemployment;
- the fortunes of local industry.

As the population becomes wealthier and better educated, the demand for even more educational facilities, leisure centres and other facilities rises. Expectations may also rise as people expect better provision of facilities in their private sector to be reflected in the public sector. These trends are encouraged by a larger disposable income as living standards rise, families become smaller and more wives work. Services need to be adjusted to meet the constant changes in demand.

Demographic trends can be charted very accurately in the short and medium term. Such charting is important for many non-profit institutions because it enables them to predict the size of their potential market. Although demographic trends may be overtaken by other changes, such as shifts in the geographical location or the age participation rate, they still provide the underlying trend.

Cultural Factors

Marketing needs to take account of the basic beliefs in a particular society. Within a society, there will be subcultures of people with shared values and these may influence the work of non-profit organisations – they may even be chosen as target markets. People also have secondary beliefs, which are open to change. A core belief may be in the institution of marriage, while the view that people should marry early is a secondary belief. Shifts in cultural values encouraging women to have careers before marriage have led to the acceptance of people marrying later and having children when they are older.

Societies' attitudes to pleasure seeking, to helping others, to government institutions and to their natural surroundings are all matters for consideration by marketing. Schools, for example, will influence and be influenced by societies' attitudes and behaviour. Marketing an image of an authoritarian regime may not be popular among pupils, parents or local politicians in one society or subculture, while it may be supported by another.

6.3 **Technological Factors**

The development of new products changes, among other things, the way in which people work. Hospitals, for example, use a vast array of modern equipment and are major purchasers of modern technology. In marketing terms, institutions will often want to emphasise their use of modern equipment and technologies, particularly in comparison to their competitors.

Activity 3

What does the term 'technology' mean to you? Consider the types of technological resources available to you.

6.4 **Economic Factors**

Markets require money as well as people. Disposable income and purchasing power depend on a range of variables, such as changes in real income, levels of savings and debt, and the availability of credit. The non-profit sector can be greatly affected by changes in disposable income, although the effects may not be as immediately obvious as in the private sector.

When purchasing power is reduced, spending on longer term capital items slows down. Consumers will put off moving house, buying a new car or new furniture; they will continue to buy food and other necessities. Non-profit hospitals and schools may see little change in their funding in the short term, but if the reduction in spending power is a reflection of a downturn in the national economy, their funding will be reduced in the longer term.

Areas of the non-profit sector that may not be considered necessities, such as museums, art galleries and charities, may feel an immediate effect. People may be more reluctant to travel to museums and art galleries if their spending power is reduced, and may not be willing to pay any entrance fee. Charities may be faced with reduced donations if such gifts are considered to be a luxury.

Monetary and fiscal policies affect people's disposable income because it is influenced by such factors as levels of interest rates and inflation. High levels of inflation will reduce people's real income as opposed to money income, while high interest rates will mean that a greater proportion of people's real income will be spent on servicing their debts, such as mortgages and credit purchasing, and therefore less will be available for other purposes. The same will be true of high levels of taxation.

If a rise in the level of taxation is not a reflection of a general downturn in the economy, but is a reflection of government decisions to spend more on services, then non-profit institutions such as those in education and health may benefit. This is a matter of policy and it will affect all local government services.

The distribution of income will also be important for the non-profit sector. If charities depend on donations from the wealthier part of the population, changes in the economy may not affect them to the same extent as it would if they depended on the poorer groups. Rises in unemployment may affect lower income groups in particular and cause a reduction in their disposable income. This may not greatly affect donations to charities or the funding of public sector institutions, but it may increase the demand for other public sector services, such as social services and unemployment benefits.

In general terms, as people's income rises, the percentage spent on food and necessities declines while spending on relative luxuries, such as transport, recreation and travel, increases. This increase includes savings and donations to charities, as well as a demand for improved education and health services. This increased demand may result in an increase in private education and health services, and the effect that this has on the public sector will depend on the political situation.

Activity 4

Consider the importance of financial restraint on marketing, the methods of reducing the impact of this, and the use of measures of efficiency in relation to any organisation you know.

6.5 Political Factors

Non-profit organisations in the public sector are greatly influenced by the political and legal environment. The way in which schools and hospitals are governed depends on Acts of Parliament and local control. While legislation affects the private sector to some extent – for example, by protecting consumers and society, and controlling monopolies – the non-profit sector is controlled to a considerable extent by legislation. Public corporations are set up by governments, education strategy is decided by legislation, and charitable status is controlled by law.

The long- or medium-term marketing plan of a non-profit organisation may be turned upside down by a new law or local authority decision. A secondary school, for example, may have its whole character changed by a reorganisation scheme. The size of the school may be changed, its sixth form status may be removed and its budget may be altered. The actual level of self-government of secondary schools is usually determined by law, so that unlike a private sector institution, a school may not have control over its own future. A school may also have its curriculum altered by changes in national or local policy, so that its actual 'product' is controlled by politics. These factors will influence not only what is marketed by the school, but may also influence the way in which marketing is carried out.

Activity 5

What impact would you expect the following to have on school sixth forms and colleges of further education?

- training and enterprise councils;
- local management of schools and further education;
- training credits;
- LEA policy on education for the 16–19 age group.

6.6 Competition

Non-profit organisations need to know who their competitors are as they will affect the way in which the organisations operate. For example, if a school suffers from a relatively poor image compared with others in its area, this may not matter at a time when the numbers of potential pupils are high, but it will matter when these numbers fall. Even when schools are full, a comparatively good reputation may help if a school wants to select its pupils or is looking for support to develop its facilities.

Non-profit sector institutions are in competition for public funds. There are limited funds for schools, hospitals, libraries, museums, art galleries, social services, housing, leisure services and so on. Each public sector has to compete with other sectors, and each institution has to compete with other institutions in the same sector, for its share of the funding. Charities are in competition in rather the same way. As with institutions, some charities are more able to present themselves as generally more worthwhile than others. It can be argued that it is easier to market and advertise charities concerned with poverty, children and animals, than charities specialising in relatively obscure illnesses or concerned with abstract ideals.

Activity 6

Consider how far competition is a factor in any non-profit organisation you know. List the competitors you can identify.

Such differences can be offset by developing a good image and a reputation for effectiveness, and by concentrating on those aspects which are attractive to clients. Charities involved with environmental issues, for example, may need to concentrate on particular issues, such as the survival of the rain forests, whales or dolphins, or problems of nuclear pollution.

Activity 7

'The manager of a National Health Service district needs to be especially sensitive and politically aware, for in order to succeed he has to carry all the different constituents with him.

As well as having the support of the medical profession it is vital that he has the support, or at the minimum not the opposition, of the public and political parties represented on his controlling committee. Every businessman is well aware of the problems of balancing the often conflicting demands of the shareholders, employees, customers and inhabitants of the areas in which they operate. The balancing of such demands is, for all of us, a necessary management skill. For a businessman, however, the opposition of one of these groups may lead to difficulties, but is unlikely to stop him stone cold dead in the water. It is this sort of structural difficulty which made the health management task such a fascinating and frustrating one' (John Harvey-Jones). In what ways do you think a manager in the non-profit sector can help his/her organisation to compete successfully in its market?

6.7 The Market

Non-profit organisations need to know their market, its size, its likely growth or concentration, and of course its customers. Every market has its own system of communication, as well as its own trade practice, pricing system, product service and so on. This may depend on geographical location and, particularly in the public sector, on laws and controls set by central and local government agencies.

A school's market will be the pupils and parents in its catchment area. This may have a geographical boundary, which both limits the school's possible expansion and the ability of other schools to compete, because they have their own boundary. If a system of 'free trade' is introduced, so that parents can choose which school their children attend, and the catchment areas are limited only by the ability of the children to travel, the market will change dramatically. A school will now be in competition with others in the wider catchment area.

Within an educational market, there may be schools with different curricula and methods of delivery, private schools offering a different approach to discipline, extra-curricular activities or attitudes to examinations, and so on. There will be recognised means of communication, perhaps by letters sent home via the pupils and by holding an annual school fair. As competition increases, either as a result of demographic trends or changes in the institutions in the market, the need to consider an overall marketing strategy will become increasingly important.

Activity 8

In what ways do you expect the wants and demands of your existing customers to change in the future?

The level of importance given to marketing will depend on the demand in the market. This may be low or negative, so that people actively attempt to avoid the product/service. Dental services are a good example of this, but schools and hospitals with poor reputations may fall into the same category. Services such as dental treatment, which many people would like to avoid, need positive promotion.

When there is no apparent market demand, it may be possible to develop it by linking the product/service to individual needs. Business people, for example, may not have a desire to learn a foreign language until the benefits are put to them. Conversely, there may be a latent demand; that is, consumers have a desire for something that is not satisfied by existing products/services. The demand for safer neighbourhoods, for example, may be able to be satisfied once the size of the potential market has been measured.

Where demand is declining, the marketing task is to reverse the fall. This will involve analysing the reason for the decline and determining whether demand can be restimulated through finding new markets, changing the features of the service/product on offer or by more effective communication. If the demand is irregular, the task is to alter the time pattern of demand through flexible pricing, promotion and other incentives. Museums may be overcrowded at weekends and relatively empty in the week; this pattern of attendance may be altered by offering discount arrangements in the week.

Marketing still has a challenge to face when there is full demand, since the demand has to be maintained in the face of the changing market environment and possibly increasing competition. Very popular exhibitions, national parks, and schools and hospitals may have an overfull demand that they have difficulty in coping with. Waiting lists or methods of selection may be needed to reduce demand to the required level.

6.8 SWOT Analysis

Equally as important as the external environment to an organisation's marketing plan is the knowledge of its own *s*trengths, *w*eaknesses, *o*pportunities and *t*hreats (SWOT).

A SWOT analysis helps to focus attention on the key areas in an organisation that need to be taken into account in producing a marketing plan. It should be used actively in developing a marketing strategy, building on the strengths of an organisation, redressing or allowing for the weaknesses, taking full advantage of the opportunities and meeting the threats. A SWOT analysis is a summary of the marketing audit. It highlights *internal* differential strengths and weaknesses from the customers' point of view as they relate to *external* opportunities and threats.

Strengths
An organisation may be able to identify its location as a strength if it has good communication links that enable its customers to travel to it easily. If a car is a necessary form of transport and there is limited parking space, then this is a weakness. Many strengths are as obvious as this, but listing them and then placing them in order of significance can help to identify those aspects on which the organisation should build.

Non-profit organisations may have strong management teams, particularly skilled specialists, or expert knowledge in a subject or a locality that can be developed and exploited in other areas of work. A hospital is a complex institution and if it is well managed this will be one of its strengths. A college may have specialist knowledge in particular subjects that can be applied to meet training needs. Charities concerned with helping other countries may build up expert knowledge in these countries.

Strengths may be seen in such relatively tangible ways as skills of the labour force, organisation of the services, ease of communication, layout and appearance of the buildings, and high technology equipment. They may also be seen in more abstract forms, such as the image and reputation of an organisation, or its standing compared to competitors.

Weaknesses

These will be the opposites to the strengths. A poor reputation, badly organised services, difficult communication links, a badly decorated and furnished building, these are all weaknesses that an organisation will need to redress in one way or another if it is to compete successfully in its market.

If a weakness can be identified, it may be possible to correct it. If a college is being pressed to be more marketing orientated and it knows that its management team has few marketing skills, it could appoint a marketing professional and/or provide staff training, or take other action, in order to fill this gap.

This type of weakness may arise because of a 'shifting of the goalposts' – if an organisation's environment changes, weaknesses may be exposed. If schools are given greater autonomy over their own finances as a result of legislation, this may throw up managerial weaknesses that were not significant before the change. A fall in the birth rate combined with a change in the rules to provide parents with an open choice of schools may increase the need for a school to develop a competitive edge.

Activity 9

List the strengths and weaknesses of your organisation, or of an organisation you are familiar with.

Opportunities

These may also arise because of a 'shifting of the goalposts' – exposure of a weakness may be seen as an opportunity to develop it. A weakness such as limited car parking around a college and poor communication links may be turned into an opportunity to provide the extra service of transport to students. If an organisation is working effectively in spite of its weaknesses, it may do even better if it can put some of them right.

Opportunities may be discovered by marketing research, which may reveal a part of the potential market that is untouched. A charity may have concentrated on raising money from one group of donors without realising its cause would appeal to another group. The experience of similar organisations may indicate opportunities that have not been developed. For example, a hospital may observe that another hospital is able to sell a wide range of goods in its shop and thereby raise funds for the hospital.

Threats

Competition is the most obvious threat to most organisations and it is important to identify rival providers of goods and services very precisely. Public sector organisations may compete with each other and also against the private sector. This is true of hospital services, colleges and universities, transport, and leisure and entertainment services.

Activity 10

Carry out a SWOT analysis of your own or another non-profit organisation.

The non-profit sector may be threatened by changes in the economy causing a reduction in donations and expenditure. Public sector institutions may find their funds reduced because of economic changes or policy decisions about the levels of public expenditure and the distribution of funds to particular services. Areas such as defence, education, health and social services are prone to budget cuts because they constitute such a large proportion of central government spending. In the same way, education is vulnerable to cuts in local government expenditure.

These 'internal' struggles are as much about communication within an organisation as about marketing in the sense of retaining a competitive edge. Management policy within an organisation can encourage a corporate view, so that co-operation rather than competition is encouraged, and changes in expenditure are accepted as the responsibility of the whole organisation. This can be a very different scene from the strongly competitive position of the external marketplace.

6.9 Case Study

A primary school will be greatly influenced by political decisions made by the local authority or central government. Examples include the National Curriculum, the size of entry to the school, the budget per capita and new buildings. Social factors will affect the mixture of pupils attending the school, while technology will influence the delivery of particular subjects. Social and economic factors will need to be considered in marketing the school, while its position in local education may be decided by political decisions.

Demographic trends will indicate the future demand for the school, while an increased interest in sport or leisure classes may increase the demand for the school's halls, dining room and playing fields by adult classes, clubs and societies. Attitudes towards education will affect the school's image.

The school can choose relatively cheap methods to market itself if it has limited resources. It can publicise its successes both to staff, parents and pupils, and through the local press. The deputy head can be given the task of sending material to the local newspaper. The headteacher can play a major part in representing the school, while all staff can be encouraged to use every opportunity to improve its reputation.

If advertising is used, its effectiveness can be measured by asking people whether they have seen it and how it has affected them. Advertising for pupils may not prove very cost effective, while close liaison with local nursery schools and play groups may be more expensive, in staff time at least, but more cost effective.

School sixth forms will feel the impact of the local management of schools: it will alter the relationship with the local authority and will give the school greater autonomy. Local education authority (LEA) policy on education for the 16–19 age group will be a major factor in deciding whether or not the sixth form will disappear or expand; LEA reorganisation may support or remove the sixth form as part of its strategic plan, while extra resources, buildings and equipment will encourage pupils to stay on. The primary school may obtain greater autonomy and local management, which will tend to throw a greater emphasis on marketing.

Technology is concerned with techniques for carrying out tasks: new equipment and machinery can create new ways of teaching. A primary school will apply technology in the delivery of the curricula, and in its management. Computers and information technology will tend to have an increasingly important impact on the school as equipment and programmes become available. This is true not only in the top forms of the school, but also in younger classes, and in management information systems. Overhead projectors, videos and many other forms of technology will be increasingly used together with modern equipment in specialised subjects such as science, art and craft.

A school will compete with other schools in the area, including private preparatory schools. It is competing for pupils, for resources and for recognition. Its competitors include:

- other primary schools;
- private schools;
- other local government services (in terms of resources).

The headteacher of a primary school, together with the staff, can ensure that the school has a good public image. At the same time, they will need to satisfy their governing body, the local education authority and others, such as local employers, that they are providing a high quality, cost-effective service. The school managers need to pay constant attention to all aspects of the school work, keep up with the various initiatives that arise in education and communicate the good work of the school to these groups. They can, on the one hand, provide public relations to the bodies making conflicting demands on them and, on the other hand, provide leadership and support for school staff.

The expectations of pupils and parents will rise over a period of time both in terms of levels of attainment and in terms of materials and equipment, such as computers. The demands of outside bodies will also rise and change with time. Central government and local authority demands will change as parties and policies change, and employers and secondary schools will alter their expectations of primary school-leavers.

A primary school's strengths and weaknesses may include:

Strengths	Weaknesses
High quality staff	Staff shortage
Good results	Poor results
Favourable location	Poor location
Up-to-date equipment	Out-of-date equipment
A sports hall	Lack of sports facilities
Playing fields	Lack of playing fields
Strong parent support	Little parent support

The school's opportunities and threats may include:

Opportunities	*Threats*
More resources	Budget cuts
Raising funds	Fewer funds
Competing successfully	Competition
Developing new teaching methods	Weakness of subjects and courses
Appealing to more parents and pupils	Opposition of parents and pupils
Autonomy	Autonomy

Weaknesses can be turned into opportunities; for example, by hiring sports facilities and building up a reputation in this area. Threats can be met by considering the strengths of the institution; for example, by emphasising and publicising high quality staff and good results.

7 The Marketing Mix

7.1 The Four 'Ps'

Once an organisation knows its position in relation to its market, understands its internal and external position, and has an idea of what its customers need, it can develop its marketing strategy. Organisations have four major variables that can be controlled in order to arrive at their marketing strategy. These are the product/ service produced by the organisation, its price, the way it is promoted and the place(s) through which it is made available to the consumers. These variables, the four 'Ps', constitute the marketing mix:

* product;
* price;
* place;
* promotion.

The marketing mix can be defined as the appropriate combination, in a particular set of circumstances, of the four 'Ps'. It consists of everything an organisation can do to influence the demand for its product/service. If any one of the four 'Ps', or the balance between them, is wrong, the marketing programme is likely to fail. The organisation has to answer questions such as:

* What should the product/service range be?
* What is the best pricing policy?
* How should the product/service be distributed?
* How should the product/service be sold?

Within an organisation's marketing environment, there are customer wants and needs. The organisation's abilities should be matched with these: the promotion and distribution of the products/services are concerned with reaching potential customers, while the range and price of products/services enable the organisation to meet customers' needs. An effective marketing strategy will weld the four variables together in order to satisfy customers. Ideally, this will have what can be described as a synergistic effect, so that the total combined effect will be greater than the sum of the parts (Figure 7.1).

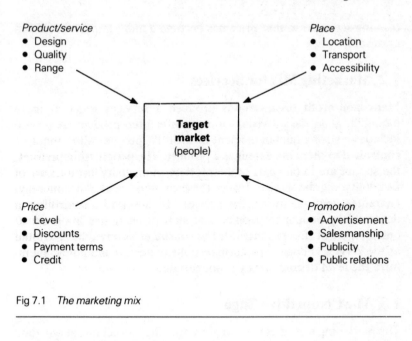

Fig 7.1   *The marketing mix*

Activity 1

How do 'people' fit into the marketing mix? How important are 'people' in the marketing of your organisation?

What happens to any one element in the marketing mix will have an effect on one or more of the others. For example, to improve the performance of a service, the quality may be raised, which may add to its cost to produce and price. On the other hand, if the service is improved, it may be more acceptable to people, leading to higher sales, economies of scale, and lower unit costs and prices.

Most markets consist of several subsidiary markets, each of which needs an appropriate marketing mix. For example, further education colleges have their main market, which may be education for the 16–19 age group, and subsidiary markets, such as research, and industrial and commercial training. These markets require different approaches to marketing management, with price, place and promotions of more or less importance in the subsidiary markets than the main one. A greater emphasis on universities raising income for themselves, for example, has encouraged the development of a marketing strategy to promote marketplace levels of payment for training services, so that price has become a more important consideration.

7.2 Marketing Mix for Services

Many non-profit organisations produce a service, which is more intangible than the provision of a manufactured product. A service includes a strong human element or fifth 'P', people, who cannot be controlled to the same extent as a product. The people who 'perform' the service are in fact part of the product – university lecturers are in fact delivering the service. Under these circumstances, it is difficult to guarantee the quality of the service. In a service, something is delivered by people to people. The staff of an organisation are as much a part of the 'product' for the consumer as any other attribute of the service. People's performance fluctuates up and down; therefore, the level of consistency is not certain.

7.3 The Competitive Edge

The marketing mix does not remain static: the correct mix at one time may not be the best combination at a later date. Products and services are improved or made obsolete, and new ones are introduced. Price structures change, and inflation, interest rates and other factors will have varied effects.

Promotional plans will need to be constantly developed and updated; the point of sale may become less satisfactory over time and alternatives may emerge. For example, the services offered by a hospital are updated as new medical techniques are developed and others become outdated. Government policies may affect pricing strategies, with charges made for certain facilities and not for others.

To retain the 'competitive edge' in a target market, an organisation must develop and communicate the differences between its offering and those of its competitors. The key to competitive positioning is to understand how members of the target market evaluate and choose among competitive institutions. For example, the target market may judge between college business studies departments by the level of information technology and other facilities they have, the type of courses they offer and their reputations (Figure 7.2).

An organisation needs to choose a marketing mix that will support and reinforce its chosen competitive position at an expenditure level it can afford. The college business studies department will need to maintain and improve its level of equipment, employ expert staff to provide good quality courses of the desired type and let the people in

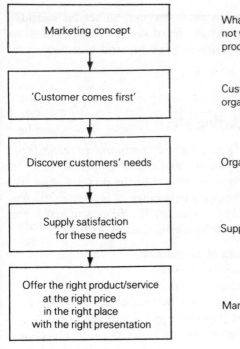

Marketing concept	What people want, not what the organisation produces
'Customer comes first'	Customer-orientated organisation
Discover customers' needs	Organise marketing research
Supply satisfaction for these needs	Supply benefits and solve problems
Offer the right product/service at the right price in the right place with the right presentation	Marketing mix

Fig 7.2   *The marketing concept*

the target market know about what it can offer. The department will of course need to have enough money to make this possible, otherwise it will have to accept a more modest programme at a lower level of spending.

Activity 2

How do you expect to retain the 'competitive edge' in your organisation?

In a non-profit organisation, price may not be important because there may not be a direct charge for a service or it may be heavily subsidised. The quality of the service and its reputation may be far more important. As consumers become more discerning, the extent to which the service matches their needs may become of paramount importance. Marketing management is concerned with the analysis, planning and control of the matching process. Successful matching depends upon customers being aware of the products/services on offer and finding them conveniently available and acceptably presented.

7.4 The Optimum Marketing Mix

Each organisation has to seek to achieve its optimum marketing mix; that is, the least amount of money and effort needed to meet its objectives. In the private sector, profit will be the primary objective, while in the public sector there may be a range of objectives, such as levels of expenditure or quality of service. The process of arriving at the optimum marketing mix can be summarised as APPEAL:

- *a*ssess the needs and desires of consumers;
- *p*roduce the right commodity or service;
- *p*rice the commodity or service successfully;
- *e*nsure that a high quality and cost-effective service is available;
- *a*dvertise and promote the product/service effectively;
- *l*aunch an efficient distribution system.

These elements can be manipulated and varied to improve the effectiveness of a marketing programme.

Activity 3

What do you understand by the 'marketing mix'? Assess the optimum marketing mix in your organisation.

Marketing strategy varies because of the differences between markets, organisations and personnel. Ideally, decisions are defined by the market and conditioned by organisational factors, so that the market defines who wants a service, where, how often and through which channels, while the organisation has strengths and weaknesses in meeting those requirements, and particular resources and attitudes. In many cases, the mix is influenced by personal reasons. A manager, for example, may have particular views about the importance of keeping prices as low as possible or about the success of advertising. If the mixture of the four 'Ps' has always been more or less the same with reasonable success, the risk of change may not be easy for long-serving managers to accept.

7.5 Manipulating the Marketing Mix

Changing the marketing mix is only worthwhile if it will result in significant customer benefits, an improvement in the cost effectiveness of supplying these benefits or the elimination of spending on activities that do not produce rewarding benefits. Varying the mix in response to changing circumstances is crucial to competitive success. As well as choosing a mix that is unique to any of its competitors, an organisation needs to monitor and improve it constantly. Any improvements should be in areas that customers rate highly, and these are likely to be areas that competitors already carry out well.

To retain the competitive edge, it is important to remember that marketing is not a series of specialist activities, but a total approach that should permeate the whole organisation. Marketing starts with the first contact with the customer. This may be a college prospectus, an advertising brochure, or it may be a telephonist or receptionist. Marketing is a set of attitudes and techniques designed to exploit the marketing situation fully and to meet competition by innovation rather than imitation.

7.6 The Non-profit Mix

The typical non-profit marketing mix will place a high emphasis on the product/service and servicing, while a low emphasis will be given to price, advertising and packaging. For example, a hospital may be more concerned with the quality of its medical practice, which is its 'product', than with pricing, advertising or 'packaging'. As hospitals become self-governing, however, they pay much more attention to these factors.

Most non-profit organisations rely on word-of-mouth opinions to establish their reputation, which is why the quality of the service is a high priority. A low or non-existent direct price is not a substitute for quality in a competitive situation. The service should come up to some level of expected performance however cheap or 'free' it may be. For example, patients may be prepared to wait for the medical attention they want and to travel distances for it, if necessary. However, in more competitive situations, the service needs to be available in a place that is convenient to the customer. In the same way, however important the service may be to the customers, they are more likely to be contented if it is well presented than if it is not.

Activity 4

Does your organisation place a higher emphasis on the service it provides than on price or advertising?

If any one of the four 'Ps' is wrong, the marketing effort may be damaged. The marketing mix can be described as the fulcrum of the marketing effort in the sense that it is the means by which influences on the market are brought to bear and it is the point that supports the move forward into action. Once an organisation has decided what business it is in, considered its strengths and weaknesses, analysed its marketing environment, and considered what products/services are required and by whom, it can then consider its marketing strategy in terms of the variables under its control.

7.7 Case Study

An orchestra depends on people for all aspects of its operation. Its 'product' consists of providing entertainment in the form of music; it may charge for its performances, promote itself in a variety of ways and perform in a variety of places, including concert theatres and halls hired for the purpose. People are needed in a number of ways in the production of the music: they are involved in the promotion and in the performances. An audience is essential in the sense that a performance can only really exist if there is one, so that the people who make up the audience are the orchestra's customers.

The orchestra can retain its competitive edge by discovering what audiences want and then providing it at a price they can afford. Marketing research can help to identify people's wants. The price may be subsidised by public funding or commercial sponsorship, but the orchestra will still be in competition with other orchestras and forms of entertainment for audiences. It will also be in competition for public funds and private sponsorship.

The marketing mix is the combination of the four 'Ps' used to market an organisation. An orchestra's marketing mix will be at its optimum when it is successful in 'selling' its services. This involves offering the right music, in the right way, at the right time and in the right place, at a price that people are able and willing to pay.

An orchestra may be more concerned with the quality of its music than with advertising performances or making a profit. However, the future of the orchestra will depend on its success, which may be measured by the size of audiences and earned income. Well targeted advertising and appropriate pricing of tickets will help to achieve these objectives.

8 Products and Services

8.1 What Is a Product/Service?

'A product is anything that can be offered to a market for attention, acquisition, use or consumption that might satisfy a want or need. It includes physical objects, services, persons, places, organisations and ideas' (Philip Kotler). This definition includes services and it is useful both to realise that they are 'products' and that there are differences between them and physical products. Whereas a product is tangible and its sale involves a change of ownership, a service is essentially intangible and does not result in the ownership of anything tangible. The production of a service may or may not be linked to a physical product, so that after-sales service, for example, is connected to a product, while a service such as the health service is not linked to a product in the same way.

All commodities and services should be produced by organisations to match customers' wants. Commodities and services can be viewed as problem solvers: they solve the customers' problems as well as being the means for achieving the organisation's objectives, and it can be argued that every product is really the packaging of a problem-solving service. This means that marketing products and services is about selling benefits, not features. People buy computers in order to solve problems and they may be more interested in the software program than the details of the hardware. Students attend a course in order to obtain a qualification or learn a skill and these benefits are more important than any tangible features that may be included.

Of course, features may be important if they help to provide benefits. When people buy a car, they not only purchase a means of transport but also other things, such as status. The features may help to provide this. In fact, competition is often not so much about the product as about the value added to it in the form of packaging, services, customer advice, financing, delivery arrangements and so on.

In considering the target market, organisations need to take account of the six 'Os':

- occupants – which individuals constitute the market?
- object – what does the market wish to buy?

- occasions – when does the market make purchases?
- organisations – who is involved in the decision to purchase?
- objectives – why does the market buy?
- operations – how does the market buy?

Activity 1

Apply the six 'Os' to the major target market of your organisation.

A non-profit institution, such as a college, needs to know who its potential students are, what qualifications and skills they want to acquire, when they want courses, whether they, their parents or their employers make decisions about courses, why they want these particular qualifications and how they will pay for them. In fact, satisfying the market has become more complex so that, for example, with the development of open and distance learning, there is a demand for more flexible delivery systems of skills and qualifications in terms of time and place.

8.2 Classification of Products/Services

- *Non-durable goods*: these are tangible goods (such as food) that are consumed rapidly and purchased frequently.
- *Durable goods*: these are tangible goods (such as television sets and clothes) that last a long time and are purchased infrequently.
- *Services*: these are intangibles (such as education and health services), in the form of activities or benefits, that are perishable and may be sought frequently or infrequently depending on their nature.

The characteristics of products and services will have a major influence on marketing strategy. Non-durable goods, for example, will usually be widely available and will be heavily advertised, to induce trials and to develop consumer loyalty. Durable goods may also be heavily advertised, perhaps because of competition, and will require personal selling. Services require quality control at every stage to establish confidence in consumers.

Activity 2

Make a list of the differences you can identify between marketing goods and marketing services.

8.3 **Services**

Services have particular characteristics that affect marketing strategy; these are important for non-profit organisations because they are often supplying services rather than products:

- *Intangibility*: services cannot be seen, tasted, felt, heard or smelt before they are bought. The customer has to have faith in the provider of the service. This is true of a patient entering hospital, a student entering a college or university and the public reaction to the police force (Figure 8.1). Tangibility can be increased by producing descriptions of the service through brochures and prospectuses, and by emphasising the benefits of the service (such as improved health in a hospital, improved qualifications or job prospects in a college) rather than describing its features.
- *Inseparability*: a service cannot exist separately from its providers. The hospital patient depends on the nurses and doctors, while

---

Fig 8.1 *The Common Purpose of The Metropolitan Police*

The Metropolitan Police has a strong tradition of service to the public and our common purpose must now be to make the quality of that service even better.

Living and working in London is a necessity for many and a pleasure for most. But it is now accompanied by the unease, and sometimes fear, caused by problems and pressures in the street and on the roads, railways and underground. Although the actual risk of being a victim of crime is low, some people live in fear, especially of violent crime.

Our service to the public is provided mostly at a local level. The first impression the public has is usually of the officer on patrol or visiting their homes or on the phone or at the front desk in the police station. The lasting impression of us – of what we say or do or write – is formed by encounters with individual officers and civil staff.

The reassurance provided by the sight of an officer on patrol and by the firmness, courtesy and kindness with which we do our job is more and more important. The more people believe in us and in our ability to succeed, the less they will feel in danger.

I recognise that it is easier for us to provide a professional service and to be compassionate, caring and, if necessary, courageous when we respond to members of the public who are victims of crime or who clearly depend on us to help them. It is more difficult, however, to uphold first class standards when we are dealing with those who have flouted the law or who are abusive, threatening and sometimes violent. Nevertheless, whatever the provocation, I expect and demand that we all do our duty to the highest standards.

students depend on lecturers and support staff for the services they are seeking.

- *Variability*: a service depends on who provides it and when and where it is provided. The particular nurses caring for a patient can affect the provision of the service as can such matters as conditions of the ward. A high quality of service can be controlled by an organisation investing in good personnel selection and training of staff, and monitoring customer satisfaction so that poor service can be detected and corrected.
- *Perishability*: services cannot be stored. If a hospital patient misses an appointment, the medical service cannot be provided and the consultant's time may be wasted. It can be argued that the service value only exists when the patient and the consultant meet. The perishability of a service can be reduced by matching supply with the demand. An appointment system for consultants and patients, or an enrolment system for students, may help to do this. If the supply of a service is scarce, part-time staff can be used or customer participation can be encouraged (patients completing their own medical records) to help to fill the gap.

It is possible to distinguish services according to whether they are people based (consultants) or equipment based (computers), whether the customer presence is necessary (dentists) or not (repair services), as well as whether the service is designed to make a profit or not.

Activity 3

How far can the main characteristics of services be applied to the police force?

8.4 Getting the Product Right

Getting the product/service right can be described as the single most important activity of marketing. If the product/service is not what customers want, no amount of promotion or price incentives will encourage them to demand it, at least more than once. If the product/service does satisfy the consumer, then:

- the demand is likely to be repeated;
- other products/services of the organisation may be demanded;
- the organisation's products/services may be recommended to other consumers.

In the non-profit sector, personal recommendation is likely to be one of the most important ways in which an organisation's reputation and image will be developed. This will depend on a high level of quality of all the products/services it provides, and it is an essential role of marketing to produce added benefits so that the products/services of the organisation can be distinguished from those of its competitors. The concept of the *unique selling proposition* (USP) refers to the features of a product/service that offer unique benefits not found in its competition. These features may include the quality of design, style or service, or the reliability of the product, or may be based on the provision of the service and its cost. With a service in particular, customers may use it initially for one reason, but return for a different one. Staffing factors may play an important part here. For example, British Airways has found from surveys carried out to investigate the factors contributing to customer satisfaction that over 60% was based on staff attitudes and level of service, while less than 40% was based on factors such as training, food and seating facilities. At the same time, 70% of the contribution to dissatisfaction was because of staff factors and 30% for other factors.

Activity 4

What are the main features of the product/service of your organisation?

The 'service' product cannot be stored, is difficult to demonstrate, cannot be resold and depends heavily on the staff 'delivering' it. The consumer is participating in a social interaction when receiving a health service or an educational service. The quality of the service may be perceived by the consumer in terms of how well the interaction is managed. This is the essential factor in 'service' product design. However carefully a training programme for company staff is designed, it will not succeed unless the trainees are happy with the way in which it is delivered by the tutors/facilitators (Figure 8.2).

Activity 5

How far can you apply the 'service' product design concept summarised in Figure 8.2 to the services of your organisation?

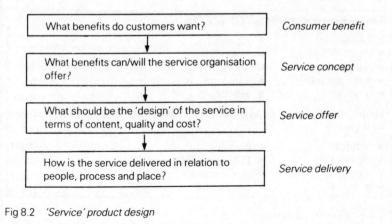

Fig 8.2 *'Service' product design*

Although a common feature of services is the role of time (labour hours, equipment hours), the product is the service, not time. The consumer judges the service on the quality of its outcome. This may depend on the expectations of the consumer, so that 'packaging' may play an important part in service design. A training course that is run by somebody well known in the specialist field and includes glossy folders and literature may be more successful than a better organised course run in a mundane style. Patients may choose a doctor who they feel is sympathetic to their problems rather than one who is expert at diagnosing them.

In offering a course, for example, a college may describe it in terms of entry requirements, structure and content, which are the areas controlled by the lecturers. For the potential student, the course is a means of achieving personal objectives, and so the way the course is promoted needs to acknowledge this. The student experience is based on the accommodation and services of the college and the content of the course, not as a syllabus but through teaching, materials and classroom organisation. Course design needs to take account of the telephonist, receptionist and enrolment procedure, as well as the content and qualifications. The course team may be able to control the syllabus and the way it is delivered, but will have more difficulty in controlling the context in which it is delivered (Figure 8.3).

Service quality is an elusive concept because it depends on the expectations of the consumers, and for complex services, such as health and education, these expectations may be different for each consumer. Total quality includes the corporate image and the technical attributes of the organisation. It is a major influence on the

The success of a service may depend on its:

- availability;
- cost;
- uniqueness;
- personal value;
- quality;
- reputation;
- fashionability;
- reliability;
- outcomes;
- delivery.

People may return to an organisation because of their perception that the staff are:

- helpful;
- cheerful;
- attentive;
- punctual;
- friendly;
- knowledgeable;
- professional;
- competent.

Fig 8.3   *A successful service*

level of demand for a service and it is a major factor in positioning an organisation in relation to its competitors.

Most organisations are concerned with total quality, with image and with reputation in the development of their product/service mix. The reputation of one product will affect that of others. A hospital will want all its departments run well, a school will aim to have every class highly thought of and a college will want every course delivered well.

For most public sector organisations, 'getting the product right' is not only concerned with achieving the correct product/service mix (Figure 8.4) and having the technical ability to deliver this 'portfolio', it is often also about having the right people with the right approach to the customers. The staff of a hospital, school, college, university, museum or gallery need to demonstrate a caring approach that is

Fig 8.4   *Product/service definition*

Product item: a single product (a university English Literature degree course)

Product line: a number of related products (all the university's English Literature degree courses)

Product group: all the product lines forming a related group of products (the university's Humanities degree courses)

Product portfolio or mix: all the products sold by an organisation (all the university's degree courses, other courses, research, consultancy and other activities)

encouraging and supportive in appropriate ways. When there are problems, staff can sympathise with customers and attempt to turn the problems into an advantage. When something goes wrong, the efforts made to 'repair the damage' may create more goodwill than if nothing had gone wrong in the first place. The mistake provides an opportunity for the staff of an organisation to show their caring, attentive, professional approach to the customer.

8.5 Life Cycle Analysis

All products/services have a life cycle in the sense that, after they are introduced, they often pass through periods of growth, then relative stability and finally decline. The performance of new products/ services typically follows an S-shaped pattern that includes four or five identifiable stages, each related to the passage of time and the level of sales or demand (Figure 8.5).

Activity 6

Draw a product life cycle graph for some of the main products/services of your organisation.

Fig 8.5 *Product life cycle*

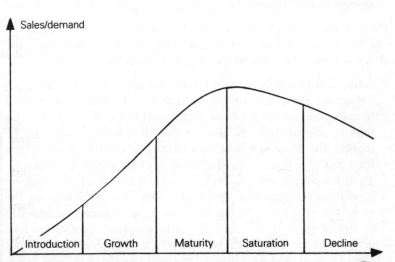

The stages in a product life cycle are:

- *introduction* – a period of slow growth as the product/service is introduced;
- *growth* – a period of rapid market acceptance;
- *maturity* – a period of slowdown in growth because the product/service has been accepted by most of the potential buyers;
- *saturation* (sometimes this is combined with maturity) – a period when there are too many competitors in a market that is no longer growing;
- *decline* – a period when performance starts a strong downward drift.

Not all products/services exhibit an S-shaped life cycle. Other possible patterns include:

- cyclical pattern – alternating high and low demand (college enrolments, votes for political parties – Figure 8.6(a));
- fad (or fashion) – a new product/service comes on to the market, attracts quick attention and is adopted with enthusiasm, peaks early and declines rapidly (aerobic classes, fashions in art – Figure 8.6(b));
- plateau pattern – demand remains steady because there is not a better alternative (GCE 'A' levels, mental health services – Figure 8.6(c));
- scalloped pattern – the product/service develops a new life cycle while in the mature stage as a result of modifications, new users, changing tastes (training programmes – Figure 8.6(d)).

The life cycle analysis is an important planning device because it enables management to focus its marketing strategy in relation to the life cycle stage of the product/service (Figure 8.7):

- Introduction: a new product/service will often be a substitute for something else either directly or indirectly. Consumers may resist the new product/service if the old one satisfied their needs. For this reason, and because the new product is not well known in the market, the demand will be slow in the introductory stage, except for a fad or fashion. The marketing strategy will be to target the groups of people who are likely to be most interested. A university or college putting on a new course may start by informing the groups most likely to be interested in it. More general groups can be described as 'innovators' or 'early adopters'. Innovators may include 'try-anything once' individuals; these people often find out about a new product without help and therefore may be safely

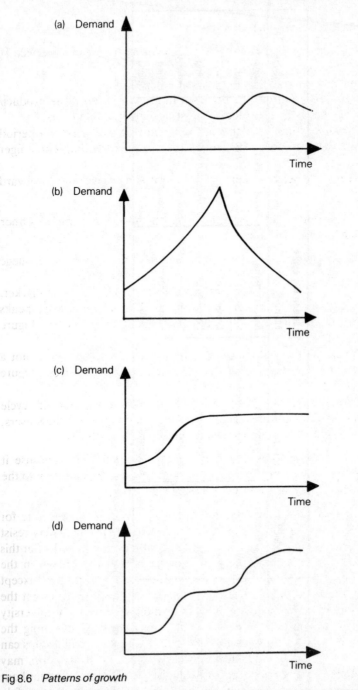

Fig 8.6 *Patterns of growth*

Product/service factor	Stage in life cycle				
	Introduction	Growth	Maturity	Saturation	Decline
Consumer	Experimental	Mass markets	Mass markets	Traditionalists	Laggards
Competition	Low	Major competitors react	Imitations	High cost of entry	High
Costs per unit	High	Rapid fall	Levelling off	Decline	Low
Promotional costs	High	Total increase	Levelling off	Diminishing returns	Falling
Pricing policy	High	Flexible	Stable	Stable	Defensive
Sales	Low	Fast growth	Slower growth	Decline	Falling
Cash flow	Negative	Moderate	High	Low	Falling

Fig 8.7   *Stages and strategies in the product life cycle*

ignored in marketing. Early adopters are more important because they may be part of the target group. If they are not convinced by the need to demand the new product/service, the introductory period may be prolonged. This group constitutes the opinion leaders, people prepared to take a risk, and they can be said to 'legitimise' the innovators.

- Growth: once the 'pilot' stage or early 'trials' are over, and assuming that they have been successful, the benefit of the product/service will have become accepted. Production difficulties will have been overcome and development costs covered, so that the product/service can be produced more cheaply than before. Increased demand means that economies of scale can have an effect. Marketing strategy will involve a wider promotion to target new customers. As competitors enter the market and spend money on promoting their product/service, awareness of the product/service is increased further and a 'bandwaggon' effect develops. The reputation of the product/service will become important both for attracting new customers and for repeat orders.
- Maturity: the product/service becomes widely accepted and competition becomes a very important element in marketing. An organisation may attempt to assume the position of market leader because it believes its product/service is of higher quality, superior to competitors' similar offerings. Some organisations may adopt marketing strategies that challenge market leaders by emphasising the advantages of their product/service. Others will be content to follow the leaders because challenging is considered to be too expensive. Effective results may be achieved without too much time and money being spent on marketing. A few organisations will search for a niche in the market where customer needs are not well met by the main competitors.
- Saturation: eventually, all the potential uses for a product/service will be exhausted and there may be too many competitors so that the market no longer grows. Maturity develops into saturation and this is often followed by decline as organisations search for new products/services to replace the old ones. In the private sector, this stage is often epitomised by price wars; in the non-profit sector, it may be characterised by cost-cutting exercises, in an attempt to reduce expenditure and to avoid increases in any charges that are made (museums, art galleries, theatres, training courses).
- Decline: as newer products/services are introduced, they may be substituted for the established offerings. Some organisations will stop producing the product/service because it is felt that the expenditure (investment) would be better used in another product

line. Decline may arise because of technical advances, or changes in fashion or taste. Decline may occur after a product/service has led a fairly short 'life' or after very many years. This depends on the nature of the product and its market. While the demand for short training courses may be subject to constant changes as technology advances, the demand for degree courses may have a long life cycle.

8.6 **Product Management**

Product life cycle analysis is a useful concept in marketing because it focuses attention on demand patterns. In considering what action can be taken at each stage, all of the four 'Ps' need to be brought into use:

- product/service – extra benefits and features may be added to a product/service at the mature stage in an attempt to compete successfully in the market and to avoid a decline in demand;
- price – (or costs) may become particularly important in the mature stage and when the market is saturated, since the organisation with the highest cost may be squeezed out;
- place – the distribution and location of the product/service may be limited to the most obvious and important channels during the introductory stage, while all possible channels may be used during the growth stage;
- promotion – will be used to create awareness of the introductory stage while it is used to create a favourable attitude towards the product/service in comparison with its competitors.

Activity 7

In what ways does the product life cycle affect the marketing strategy of the main product/service of your organisation?

Most organisations have a range of products/services on offer and product management involves making sure that there is a succession of products/services available that are at different stages of their life cycles. In this way, it is possible to ensure that there is always something to take the place of an offering that is in decline.

In Figure 8.8, the income from product/service A can help to finance the development of B, which in turn helps to finance the development of C. Maintaining long-term demand in most non-profit organisations requires the introduction of new products/services at

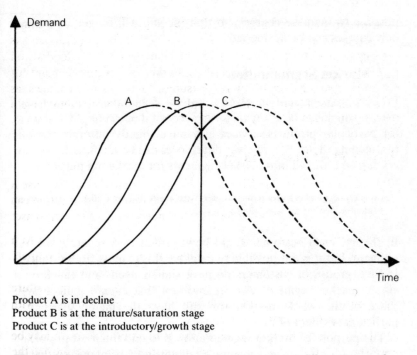

Product A is in decline
Product B is at the mature/saturation stage
Product C is at the introductory/growth stage

Fig 8.8 *Maintaining demand with products/services that are at different stages of their life cycles*

regular intervals. In the profit sector, this is important to maintain a balance between those products/services that are at an early stage of their life cycle and so are net users of cash, and those at later stages that have low costs and a high market share and so are net cash producers.

The same considerations are true in the non-profit sector where services may generate income through fees and charges, or by grants linked to levels of service. Like the private sector, non-profit organisations do not want to have to invest in new services all at one time; they need to plan and phase in innovations in order to match the budget available to them.

For example, a new computer training course will move through all the stages of the product life cycle. It will need to be promoted to target employers and employees in the introductory stage. If it is successful, the promotion can be extended to all employers in the locality. At the same time, the development cost will have been absorbed and the costs of producing extra courses will have been reduced. As acceptance of the course becomes widespread, it may be possible to increase charges, so that income will be generated and new courses can be developed.

8.7 Market Segmentation

Product management involves a careful definition of market segments, which can be a key factor in successful marketing. Customers for particular products/services may have slightly different reasons for needing them. Where clear differences can be identified, customers can be grouped into market segments for marketing purposes:

> A market segment is a group of customers with needs that are distinctive from those of other groups for the same product/service.

In theory, each customer could be regarded as a separate market segment, but it is not possible to cater for this in most circumstances. In fact, groups of customers do have similar needs and can form a viable market segment. An organisation that cannot gain a large share of the whole market can still have the major share of a particular segment of it.

The purpose of market segmentation is to find the most promising opportunities for an organisation's talents and advantages so that its strengths are of most value and its weaknesses are not important. Over-segmentation of the market may result in an organisation trying to provide products/services in too many directions, so that it loses the economies of scale. Most hospitals, for example, specialise in certain areas of medical health care so that a particular group of patients is catered for and the economies of scale can apply. Large general hospitals that do not specialise and attempt to provide all aspects of health care may find that they are attempting to offer too many services at once.

Segmentation is usually based on the characteristics or attributes of customers. These may include:

- socio-economic factors such as income and social class;
- psychological factors such as attitudes and needs;
- demographic factors such as age, sex and marital status;
- geographical factors such as country, region, urban or rural area;
- life style factors such as young 'upwardly mobile' families and well-off retired couples;
- loyalty factors such as 'brand' loyalty. Brands consist of a name, sign, symbol or design that identifies the products/services of an organisation to consumers and helps to differentiate them from those of competitors. Schools and colleges produce prospectuses,

leaflets and notepaper with logos and other design features so that pupils, parents, students and employers will immediately recognise the origin of an advertisement or communication. This can help to establish an image for the organisation, to develop loyalty and may give an immediate impression of product/service quality.

Activity 8

What is the importance of market segmentation? How can it be applied to your organisation?

Market segments must be:

- distinct and identifiable;
- relevant;
- large enough to matter;
- easily reached.

A hospital may divide its patients by type of treatment required (medical, surgical, maternity), and by sex. Preventative medical programmes may be more concerned with age and life style (smoker rather than non-smoker). Geographical location may be relevant in both cases. A hospital needs to provide a different type of service for emergencies, for maternity patients and for elderly patients, and a high quality will be achieved only by recognising the differences between these market segments.

8.8 The Pareto Effect

This describes the tendency for a small proportion of customers to account for the largest proportion of demand. This is the 20/80 or Pareto effect: 20% of customers accounting for 80% of demand. This is a shorthand method of describing an important market segment – the 'heavy users'. In such cases, the marketing decision is whether to concentrate on the heavy users or on the large number of small users. In non-profit organisations, this effect may be seen, for example, in secondary schools, where 80% of the pupils come from a few primary schools and 20% come from a wide range of others; a college may have trainees from a few large companies and others from a wide variety of organisations; most of a hospital's work may be in 20% of the total health service; a charity may receive 80% of its donations from 20% of its donors. Does the secondary school bother with links with the large number of schools supplying one or two pupils each? Does the college worry about its relations with the large number of small firms or concentrate on its efforts on the small number of large firms supplying most of the trainees? Does the hospital concentrate its resources on the heavily demanded areas of health services or attempt to cover the whole range? Does the charity promote itself only to its most important donors or to the whole public?

Activity 9

Does the Pareto effect apply in any way to your organisation?

The Pareto principle applies in many areas of management. For example, in many non-profit organisations (hospitals, schools, colleges), 80% of the budget is spent on staff salaries and wages, while 20% is spent on other costs. Similarly, marketing budgets may be divided between areas of heavy and less heavy expenditure.

8.9 The Boston Matrix

This is a classification of products/services within a portfolio linked to their cash usage. It is based on relative market share and market growth rate. The relative market share is important because the product/service share relative to its competitors indicates the extent to which it can generate cash. The larger the share, the more cash can be generated. The market growth rate indicates the cash usage of the product/service. In fast growing markets, the product/service will be a higher user of cash in order to support the expansion.

Figure 8.9 shows the main categories of products/services used in this classification. The distinctive names given to each of the four categories of products/services indicate their prospects:

- A *star* has a high market share and a high market growth in a market that is growing fast. It will tend to generate as much cash as it uses and will be self-financing. The generation of cash may not be applicable to a non-profit organisation; instead, it may be appropriate to consider levels of demand, which in marketplace circumstances could be translated into cash terms. For example, a

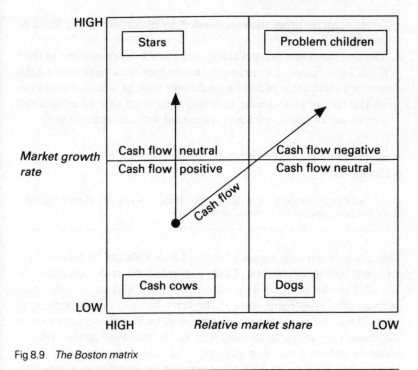

HIGH

| Stars | Problem children |

Market growth rate

Cash flow | neutral   Cash flow negative
Cash flow | positive   Cash flow neutral

Cash flow

| Cash cows | Dogs |

LOW

HIGH   *Relative market share*   LOW

Fig 8.9   *The Boston matrix*

school may have a high demand for its sixth form science classes and may have a high share of sixth form science pupils compared with competing sixth forms. The level of investment in laboratories and resources will have to keep up with increasing demand if the 'market share' is to be maintained.

- The *problem child* has a low market share and a high market growth in a market that is growing. To increase market share, it will tend to need investment and promotion, even though demand may be relatively low. For example, there may be a low share of social science pupils in a school's sixth form even though the market is growing. To increase demand, the school may have to invest in extra teachers and equipment while demand is still relatively low.
- The *cash cow* has a high market share and a low market growth in a reasonably stable market. There is little need for extra investment and promotion, so cash is generated. For example, there may be little growth in the demand for humanities classes, but a school may have a large share of the existing market. Little extra

investment or promotion is needed to maintain a high level of demand.

- The *dog* has a low market share and a low market growth; in fact, it has little future. For example, music may be a small part of the school's sixth form provision and there may be a low demand for it. The cost of maintaining staff and equipment may be considered a poor use of resources when compared with the alternatives.

Activity 10

Identify your organisation's 'stars' and 'dogs'. Show the position of your organisation's products/services on a Boston matrix diagram.

This analysis can indicate which type of policy should be followed for different products/services. Cash generated by cash cows can be invested in the stars or in selected problem children, which could become stars (the 'rising stars'). The stars, in turn, may become cash cows. It may be possible to save some dogs by identifying segments of the market on which to concentrate, or by improved productivity in order to reduce costs. For example, the school may save its music provision by linking up with other schools, by employing a part-time teacher for a limited number of hours or by concentrating on one music examination instead of several. At the same time, the fact that there may be little need to put extra resources into humanities enables the school to invest in developing social sciences while maintaining its investment in sciences.

8.10 The Ansoff Matrix

This is a way of showing the four main product/service marketing strategies (Figure 8.10):

- *market penetration*, which involves either increasing sales to existing users or finding new customers in the same market;
- *product development*, which involves modifying the product/ service in terms of such factors as quality and performance;
- *market extension*, which involves either finding new uses for the product/service and thus opening new markets, or taking the product/service into entirely new markets;
- *diversification*, which involves both product development and market extension.

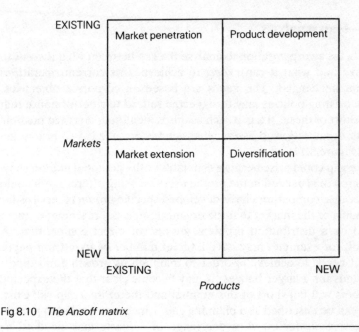

Fig 8.10 *The Ansoff matrix*

Non-profit organisations can apply these strategies in their marketing plans. For example, a charity looking for more donations may extend its promotional campaign to new potential donors in the same market, say people in a particular location such as London, or families in a particular socio-economic group. Alternatively, the charity may decide to modify its message in some way in order to extend its appeal; for example, by emphasising the support it provides for children, or by highlighting the needs of a particular country. In the same way, the charity may look for donors in entirely new markets, in areas or among people it has not considered before. It may both modify its message and extend its activities into new markets in order to diversify its 'service' and increase donations.

Activity 11

Apply the ideas expressed in the Ansoff matrix to the marketing strategy of your organisation.

8.11 Gap Analysis

This helps an organisation to analyse the gap between what it *needs* to achieve and what it can *expect* to achieve if its current operations remain unchanged. The needs are based on corporate objectives, while existing policies may be expected to lead to a performance that falls short of these. If a gap such as this is identified, it is then possible for an organisation to assess what actions are needed to bridge the gap (Figure 8.11).

The gap could arise because estimates of the potential market show that growth is needed in the product/service being offered; or it could be because competitors have developed specific products/services for segments of the market that the organisation is not reaching; or there could be a distribution problem, or one of direct competition. A school, for example, may have a target number of sixth form pupils that it needs to achieve in order to maintain its growth and support demands for a larger budget. It may become clear that the expected numbers will fall short of this number and therefore a gap will exist. This can be described as a planning gap, which may be due to present marketing strategies. A wider range of subjects may need to be offered in more combinations and information on this may need to be widely distributed in the school catchment area. In general, the image of the sixth form may need to be presented in comparison to other sixth forms, by publicising good examination results and high standards of equipment, and organising open days and induction courses.

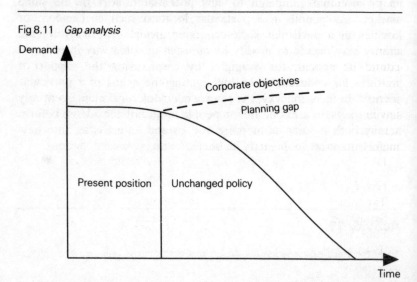

Fig 8.11 *Gap analysis*

Activity 12

Can you identify a gap in your organisation between what it needs to achieve and what it can expect to achieve?

Gap analysis can help an organisation to examine its current marketing position and the strategies that can be followed to improve its position in line with overall corporate objectives. These include all the strategies involved in consideration of life cycle analysis, the Boston matrix, the Ansoff matrix and in product/service management:

- product/service development;
- market segmentation;
- product range extension;
- market extension;
- diversification;
- product reformulation;
- market penetration;
- new product development.

8.12 Case Study

The target market for the police force is the general public. The major objective that the public will demand from the police is security and peace of mind. This is a constant demand but becomes more concentrated at particular times, such as times of disorder and when a crime has been committed. The purchase of police services is controlled by central government, local authorities and police committees. These organisations will decide on the resourcing of police forces. There is a demand for law and order, which can be met by having an efficient police force. The general demand for police services will be decided by policy on law and order, while individual members of the public make demands by direct contact.

Differences in marketing goods against marketing services:

Goods	*Services*
Tangible	Intangible
Separable	Inseparable
Standard	Variable
'Permanent'	Perishable

The police force provides a public service: all of the characteristics of other services can be applied to it. The service is intangible and the public has to have confidence that the police force is providing the correct service. The service does not exist separately to police officers, and the service depends on who provides it at a particular time and place. Individual police officers can affect the way in which the service is provided. The service provided by the police force cannot be stored, and it only exists when it is being provided.

The public, as customers of the police force, want security and peace of mind, and the police force will attempt to provide these services to the best of its ability, given limited resources. Services such as patrols, protection, detection and so on will be given or offered according to the needs of the public. The way these services are delivered will vary over time, so that the 'bobby on the beat' may be replaced by patrol cars in certain areas, and electronic surveillance of traffic flow may replace police personnel.

Foot patrols provided by police have levelled off in importance in the last 30 years and have fallen as compared with motorised patrols (Figure 8.12). At the same time, security patrols of property have been taken over by private security companies.

The drop in foot patrols has affected the direct contact that the police have with local people and attempts have been made to compensate for this, by establishing home beat and community officers to provide a link with local people. At the same time, patrol cars can maintain the 'visibility' of the police force, even if there is no direct contact with the public.

The police force can segment its market into age groups, activity

Fig 8.12   *Changes in services provided by the police force*

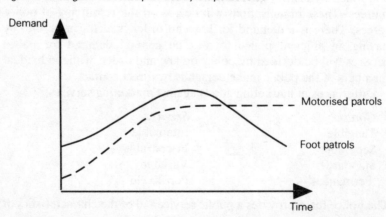

groups and of course into criminals and non-criminals. Crowd control at meetings, football matches and demonstrations forms an important segment of police work, for which special training is given. By identifying market segments, the police force can concentrate the appropriate resources and expertise into these areas.

Most police work will be with a relatively small proportion of the public and in general terms, while in terms of traffic offences and in terms of criminals and non-criminals the Pareto effect will be relevant. The police service is labour intensive so that the 80/20 split will be true of expenditure on staff salaries as against other forms of expenditure.

Police service 'stars' may be considered to be such services as high level security operations, which have a high market share and a relatively high profile (Figure 8.13). A 'dog' may be, say, burglary where successful detection is low even though it is a growing crime and the lack of success promotes a relatively poor public image of the police force. Special security contracts may earn extra 'cash', while foot patrols may be felt to be too costly to continue in most areas.

Fig 8.13 *Boston matrix in relation to police services*

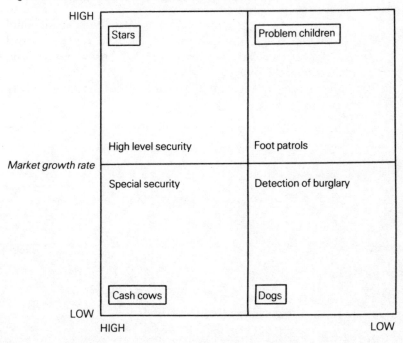

The police force can develop its services by the use of modern technology. It can penetrate new markets in areas such as computer fraud, and where new laws are made; extend the use of existing services, such as motorway patrols providing traffic information; and diversify services by the use of helicopters, as well as cars, for control and detection purposes.

As the population changes and becomes more affluent, the expectations of the public will alter in terms of the service expected from the police force. The comforting sight of the 'bobby on the beat' may be replaced to some extent by a prompt response to emergency calls or an improved detection rate. A growing gap between the number of crimes and their detection may reduce the confidence of the public.

9 Price

9.1 Introduction

Price could be considered unimportant in the marketing strategy of a non-profit organisation because often a service is provided 'free' of charge or, if a charge is made, it may represent a relatively small part of the total cost. However, there is a 'cost' or a 'price' for all goods and services whether provided by the profit or non-profit sector. The provision of a 'free' service or a subsidised service involves just as many strategic marketing decisions as the provision of a service at a profit. In one way or another, the cost of a service has to be met. While the National Health Service is 'free' at the 'point of sale', the costs of providing the service have to be covered by taxation and national insurance. The decision not to charge at the point of sale is based on a policy that price should not be a factor in determining patients' ability to receive health care. In the same way, the decision to charge directly for eye tests and spectacles is based on a policy concerned with raising revenue for this service, and on the fact that most people are able and willing to pay for this service and the product (spectacles and contact lenses) attached to it.

Consideration of the environment in which an organisation operates is an essential element in all pricing policies. For political or social reasons, non-profit organisations may not charge for products/ services, charge a subsidised price, or charge a full commercial, profitable price. For example, health and education charges may be kept at zero or as low as possible to permit wide use of these services, while traffic parking fines may be kept high to discourage traffic in the inner cities, and hospital shops may charge economic prices to provide revenue for the service.

Activity 1

What part does price play in your organisation?

These are matters of policy that ultimately refer back to laws and

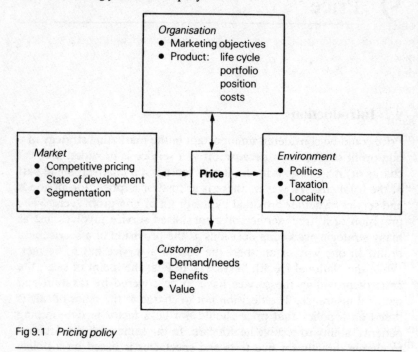

Fig 9.1 *Pricing policy*

regulations that reflect political and social ideas about how products/ services should be made available to consumers. These ideas will change over a period of time, as will policies. The emphasis may alter to charging for aspects of the service, such as dentistry in the health service and training programmes for industry arranged by universities and colleges; or to moving non-profit organisations into the profit-making sector (by 'privatising', for example, services such as steel production and gas supply) where charges may be based on profit.

In all these cases, decisions on price are based on factors that can be grouped into four main areas (Figure 9.1):

- those under the control of the organisation itself;
- those that operate in the market in which the organisation operates;
- those influenced by customers' needs;
- those determined by the marketing environment.

9.2 Pricing Policy

Marketing Objectives
Within an organisation, prices will be determined by the marketing

objectives. The price of a product/service is only one element in the marketing mix and it has to relate to all the other influences in the mix. The price must be consistent with the total marketing strategy devised for the product/service. If the marketing objective is to maximise the use of beds in a hospital, charging a high price for them is unlikely to help in the achievement of this objective. On the other hand, if an objective is to maximise revenue for a few high quality private rooms in a hospital, charging a high price for them may be the correct strategy.

The marketing objectives of an organisation might emphasise the importance of making the best use of available resources. In the first case above, prices might be kept as low as possible to encourage use of the service. In the second case, price might be used to raise revenue (or 'cash cows') that can be invested in expansion.

Product/Service Life Cycle
Pricing strategy will depend to a great extent on the product/service life cycle. In the introductory and high growth phase, demand grows fast and the product might be in short supply. At the same time, price is not likely to be the most important factor for the consumer, so there is an opportunity for the organisation to charge high prices, which will help to recover research and development costs. For example, universities can take advantage of this when they charge industry for the application of research funding.

At the mature stage of the life cycle, it may be sensible to reduce the price of a product/service to maintain or increase the share of the market. At the saturation and decline stage, price may be raised again to create a 'cash cow' with an established market, providing that market share and sales volume do not fall too quickly before a new or replacement product/service has been introduced.

For example, a university may have developed a high technology application for industry that is considered to be a brilliant innovation. The university can charge a high price initially, reducing it as the development costs are covered and the early demand is largely met, to encourage use by less enthusiastic companies. As competition develops from other universities and private suppliers, the price may be reduced further to maintain market share. As newer technology develops, the demand may decline and the university may raise prices in an attempt to obtain revenue to help development and research into new applications.

The Organisation's Portfolio
The price of a product/service may be influenced by the price of other

goods and services in the organisation's portfolio. The organisation can decide to sell a product/service at a loss in order to develop the market; that is, the product/service is a 'loss leader'. A university may decide that its new high technology application should be used in this way. It may be priced only to cover costs, or even at a lower price, so that it is impossible for commercial firms to compete while the expertise of the university is becoming established. The companies using this application may then be charged a full commercial price for after-sales service, for further features or for other services and expertise available from the university's 'portfolio' of research and consultancy programmes.

Product/Service Positioning

It is important for non-profit organisations to position their products/ services correctly in the market and price them accordingly. If a university or college training course is to be taken seriously by commercial employers, then it has to be of high quality with an appropriately high price. If the price is fixed at too low a level, the employers may wonder what is wrong with the training course. On the other hand, if employers become used to high quality, cheap courses from universities and colleges, they may expect all services from the university or college to be equally cheap, and although this will increase demand for those services, it will preclude any possibility of earning any income (profit or surplus) from these activities. However, if the cost of training courses represents a very small part of the employers' spending, they will be less concerned with the price of such courses and more concerned with the quality. In such circumstances, there is little point in universities and colleges providing cheap courses. They will need to concentrate on quality and set their prices accordingly.

Costs

Prices are often arrived at by a cost-plus process, particularly in non-profit organisations. A reason for this is that there is less uncertainty about costs than there is about demand and it is easy to arrive at a price by adding, say, 10% or 20% to the costs. At the same time, it is not necessary to make frequent changes to price in response to demand changes. It is also considered to be a 'fair' system of pricing in the non-profit sector because the sellers make a fair return while not taking advantage of buyers when there are shortages because of large demand or short supply.

There may be elements of this process in charging for eye testing and spectacles, and for dental services and false teeth.

Universities and colleges will often price their training courses for industry, and their research and consulting charges on a cost-plus basis. The costs are calculated and then a percentage or 'mark-up' is added to arrive at a price. The costs may be 'total' costs, variable costs, fixed costs or marginal costs. Variable costs vary directly with the level of output, so that the greater the number of training courses, the higher the costs in the form of staff and materials. Fixed costs do not vary directly with the level of output: they are overheads in the form of accommodation, heating, management and financial costs. It can be argued that a room has to be provided with heating and lighting whether there are three hours of courses arranged in one day or eight hours. Total costs are the sum of the fixed and variable costs for any level of output.

Price can be based on any one of these costs. It can be argued that total costs (plus a little) set the minimum price that can be charged if a profit is to be made. Non-profit organisations may decide to cover only variable costs in their charges for training courses on the argument that the fixed costs have to be covered anyway. The accommodation and equipment is already available for the 'mainstream' education courses of the university or college and therefore the extra costs for organising training courses are the only ones that need to be covered. 'Loss leaders' are often based on a price to cover fixed costs with the variable costs subsidised by other sources of revenue.

An alternative approach to costing is to consider only marginal costs. These are the costs of producing extra units of output; the marginal cost is the cost of producing one more unit – for example, the cost of organising one more hour of a training course. In determining prices, the fixed costs, which are incurred independently of the level of output, are ignored on the grounds that any price that is in excess of the unit marginal cost will make a contribution to these fixed costs. If the marginal costs of organising an extra hour of a training course are more than covered, then this contribution to fixed costs can be achieved. It may be, for example, that the fixed cost allocated to organising an extra hour of a training course is £20, variable or in this case marginal cost is £30 and total cost is £50. The price charged to make a surplus would need to be over £50, but it may be argued that all the fixed costs have already been covered, including the development and 'setting up' costs, and therefore only the marginal costs need to be covered, so the price is set at, say, £35. This provides a £5 contribution to fixed costs. In practice, it may be that the university or college only considers a proportion of the staff and materials cost because there is little idea of actual fixed costs and

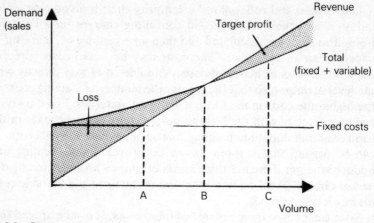

Fig 9.2   *Break-even analysis*

how to allocate a proportion of these to an existing training hour.

Activity 2

What is the pricing policy of your organisation? How important are costs in arriving at your organisation's prices?

Break-even Analysis

One way of considering this cost-orientated approach is through break-even analysis. This shows where fixed costs are covered and where all costs are covered at the 'break-even' point. It may be useful in helping to understand the relationship between different kinds of costs.

In Figure 9.2, fixed costs are shown as a horizontal line and all other costs are allocated on a cost per unit basis to produce an ascending curve. At point A, revenue covers only fixed costs; at point B, all costs are covered and only additional sales will produce net profit; at point C, profit is being achieved. By calculating its costs and deciding on its pricing policy, a non-profit organisation can pick the point on a break-even graph at which it will base its price. It should then know whether it is making a loss, a profit or breaking even.

In most organisations, there will not be a break-even point so much as a break-even area. The analysis tends to assume that, at a given price, a given number of products will be sold, but in reality the quantity sold will be dependent to some extent on the price charged.

9.3 The Influence of the Market on Price

The problem with a cost-orientated pricing policy is that price may be established independently of the rest of the marketing mix rather than as an intrinsic element of it. The price may not be raised often enough to capitalise on market changes or be sufficiently varied to take account of market segments.

Pricing strategy will depend on the type of market in which the product/service is involved. If there is pure competition in the market, there will be many buyers and sellers with a homogeneous product/service, and one price. If an organisation puts a high price on its product/service, customers will not buy it because there are plenty of other sellers. If an organisation lowers its price below that of everybody else, competition will lower the price in order to compete. This will be as true for non-profit organisations as for profit-making companies. In a very competitive market, the non-profit organisation will not be able to charge a higher price than everybody else or it will lose customers. If it sets its charges below those of everybody else, it may face a demand it cannot cope with until competitors also reduce theirs.

At the other extreme, if a non-profit organisation has a monopoly on the sale of a product/service, it can set whatever price it likes to match the desired level of demand. In other market conditions, the non-profit organisation will again have to take the conditions of supply and demand into account.

Other things being equal, a high price will tend to reduce demand while a low price will tend to increase demand. In Figure 9.3(a), a high price (P2) will lead to a lower demand (Q2) than a lower price (P1 and Q1). Demand may be very responsive to changes in price (that is, elastic) or relatively unresponsive to changes in price (that is, inelastic). In Figure 9.3(b), a small change in price (P1 to P2) leads to a less than proportionate change in demand (Q1 to Q2) and the price elasticity of demand is low. In Figure 9.3(c), a small change in price (P1 to P2) leads to a more than proportionate change in demand and the price elasticity of demand is relatively high.

In a competitive market, the price elasticity of demand will tend to be relatively high (or elastic); if the competition is more limited, the price elasticity of demand will be relatively low (or inelastic) and the organisation may be able to raise prices without greatly reducing demand. Considerations such as these will affect the use of price skimming or price penetration policies.

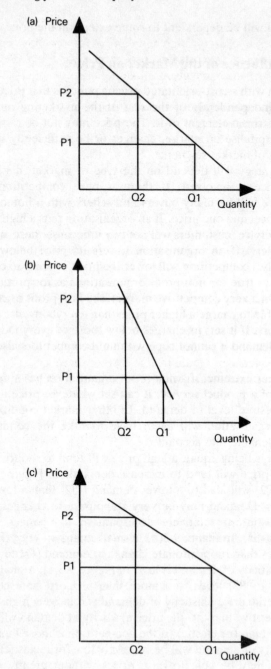

Fig 9.3 *Price and demand*

Price Skimming Policy
This is a policy of charging high initial prices for a product/service and then lowering prices as costs fall. An organisation has to estimate the highest price it can charge given available substitutes for the product/service.

The circumstances under which a skimming policy is likely to be successful include where:

- a high initial price will not attract competitors;
- the high price supports the image of a good quality product/service;
- the price elasticity of demand is likely to be low or inelastic;
- the market will have a segment that accepts high prices.

A non-profit organisation developing an innovative product/service ahead of competition might apply this policy to help to recover research and development costs. This could be in research and consultancy to industry, or in selling training programmes or developing new products.

Price Penetration Policy
This is a policy of charging a low initial price in order to attract a large number of buyers and obtain a large market share.

The circumstances under which this policy is likely to be successful include where:

- the low price stimulates market growth;
- the low price discourages actual and potential competition;
- the price elasticity of demand is likely to be high so that the market is price sensitive;
- the market does not have a distinct price–market segment.

This policy may be considered if there is a possibility of attracting a large demand in order to achieve the economies of scale. A popular training programme may be felt to have a large demand, providing a low price is charged so that the market can be effectively penetrated.

Activity 3

Consider how price skimming and price penetration policies are used in your organisation or one you are familiar with.

A mixed policy may also be followed, with a high initial price being reduced quickly in order to discourage competition (Figure 9.4).

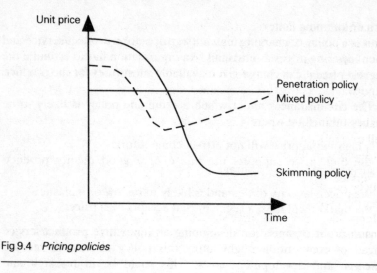

Fig 9.4   *Pricing policies*

Development and Segmentation

Price within a market may be based on the 'going rate' set by competitors. This will depend on the state of development of the product. (This has already been discussed with reference to the product life cycle.) If a non-profit organisation has a product/service for which it wants to charge in an already established market, it will need to consider existing charges, which it may in fact use as a starting point for setting a price. There may also be market segments that need to be taken into account. Private sector employers, for example, may be charged fully for a college service, while local government officers and existing students may be charged on a marginal cost basis.

9.4 The Influence of the Customer on Price

It can be argued that ultimately it is the consumer who will decide whether the price of a product/service is at the correct level. When arriving at a price for a product/service, an organisation must consider consumers' perceptions of price and how these influence consumers' buying decisions. When consumers buy a product/service, they exchange something of value, the price, to obtain something of value, the benefits they will receive from the product/service.

Effective consumer-orientated pricing involves understanding what value the consumer places on the benefits received and setting a price consistent with this value. The marketing-orientated approach to price is based on customers' perceptions. The customer's costs may be a money payment, the price, or other 'sacrifices'. A perceived cost for a consumer is any negative outcome of a proposed exchange. The 'sacrifices' or 'negative outcomes' may include problems of obtaining a service, such as waiting for it or having to travel to obtain it. In the same way, benefits for a consumer may include not only the actual service but also other factors, such as the ease of obtaining it, the quality of it and the way it is provided. All services can be provided well or badly, in a welcoming manner or only with difficulty, from the consumers' point of view. Unemployment benefits may be provided in such a way as to discourage people from obtaining them. People may be put off symphony concerts because of the formality involved – the price may not be the only obstacle.

It can be argued that price should reflect the perceived value to the consumer and, therefore, an organisation should build up the perceived value of a product/service if it wants to charge a higher price. This may be a matter of 'esteem' – the value in which a product/service is held. Scarce objects, such as works of art, may fall into this category. An art gallery may be able to charge more for an exhibition of a very famous artist than for a less famous one.

The most important value for the customer is the 'use value'. Unless customers have a use for a product/service and value it at a level that provides a satisfactory margin of profit or revenue to the supplier, the supplier will not be able to continue to provide the product/service. In the same way, 'negative esteem' value means that the price is not in line with the qualities perceived by the consumer. It can be argued that for consumers, in areas of uncertainty, price is an indication of quality.

9.5 The Influence of the Environment on Price

A non-profit organisation has to take into account the influence of economic, political and social factors on the prices it is able to charge. The market price may be directly regulated by central or local government. The tuition fees charged (or not charged) in schools, colleges and universities may be controlled in this way. Children and young people under 18 may not be charged anything for state-controlled education provision, while adults may be charged different amounts according to their circumstances. This is an important issue for non-profit organisations. Although in some areas of their work, such as hospital shops or the provision of training programmes to industry, they may be working in an open market subject to competition from other profit-making and non-profit making organisations, in other areas, often in the mainstream of their work, they are limited and controlled in their approach to pricing.

This control reflects political and social policies about such matters as access to health services, education, museums and art galleries. The provision of a 'free' library service is a result of political and social policy. It would be possible to organise a library service on fully economic lines, but the charges involved would limit access. These political and social decisions mean that non-profit organisations may find their position on price governed or changed by external regulation. They also mean that non-profit organisations are not free to follow marketplace guidelines on the provision of their products/services.

The product/service life cycle approach may indicate without doubt that a particular service is in decline and needs to be phased out. This may not be felt to be in the public interest. For example, the number of engineering students may fall to a point where it is hard for a college or university to justify, on economic grounds, the continuation of engineering courses and the use of costly equipment and materials. It may be in the public interest, however, for these courses to continue, even with small numbers. The taxation system may be used to fund the continuation of these courses even though marketing research shows that the numbers of students are not likely to increase. The system, both national and local, can be used in this way to support political decisions. In non-profit organisations, these considerations will predominate over the economic realities.

Activity 4

What are the main influences on the price of services in your organisation?

9.6 Pricing Objectives

All organisations have to decide on their pricing objectives. Are these to maximise profits, to increase usage, or to meet certain political or social aims? They also need to decide on pricing strategy. Is this based on costs, on consumer demand or on competition? Non-profit organisations may have alternative objectives, perhaps even in different sections of the organisation, or at different times in response to political and social policy.

Objectives may include the following:

- Maximum usage of the facilities available to the organisation. Museums may want to encourage as many visitors as possible and may, therefore, not wish to discourage them by charging an entrance fee. There may be a target audience in a theatre or concert hall, so that prices and promotion are designed to achieve just-full capacity.
- Funding maximisation may be desired to maintain or increase expenditures on staff and programmes. Many non-profit institutions, such as schools, museums and libraries, will have this as an objective, which they may try to achieve by showing that they are offering a high quality, cost-effective and necessary service.
- Revenue maximisation may be an objective in order to give the impression of efficiency and effectiveness. Prices may be charged whenever possible and set as high as possible in, for example, a museum (the souvenir shop) or at a college (training programmes).
- Full or partial cost recovery may be an objective. Training programmes may be priced to cover full costs or part of the costs. On a wider scale, the aim may be to keep the annual deficit of an institution from exceeding a certain level, so that charges are made where possible to maintain the gap between revenue and expenditure at this agreed amount.

9.7 Price Discrimination

Pricing objectives may lead to the introduction of price discrimination. This is selling a product/service at two or more different prices. This is common practice with entry charges to museums and art galleries, where students and pensioners are often charged less than everyone else. In the same way, children and pregnant women may receive free dental services while everybody else pays.

For price discrimination to be possible, there has to be clear segments in the market, such as children, students and pensioners, and there must be no possibility that the lower priced segments can sell the product/service to the higher priced group. As well as setting different prices for groups of customers, price discrimination can be based on other factors.

Different versions of the same product/service can be priced differently. When a service is provided, this may lead to different prices; for example, a training course delivered on a week-day may be cheaper than the same course at the weekend. The location may also be a factor, so that theatres charge more for the front of the stalls than the back. Different prices may also be charged in different parts of the country, to reflect local wages and perceived value.

Promotional pricing is a form of price discrimination over time. A lower price may be charged for a period in an attempt to stimulate demand. This may take the form of cash rebates, special events or subscription systems. Art galleries promote subscription systems such as 'Friends of the Royal Academy' who can obtain a price rebate on exhibitions; theatres and orchestras provide cheaper tickets for particular performances, possibly matinées.

Trade, quantity and cash discounts are a common feature of pricing policy. Non-profit organisations use these and every other technique in areas where they charge for their services. Discounts for large orders may be offered to encourage larger purchases than might otherwise be made. Cash discounts may be offered in return for prompt payment.

9.8 Pricing Services

Many non-profit organisations offer services rather than products, and these have their own special factors to consider. Services are perishable and special price offers may be made in order to use spare capacity. The services of skilled trainers cannot be 'stored', they must be fully utilised now or their time will be wasted. Training courses may be offered at a low price for a period of time to at least keep the trainers fully occupied and bring in some revenue.

Consumers may be able to delay or postpone the use of a service or perform it themselves. For example, instead of attending a language evening class, adult students can postpone learning the language or learn through books and cassette tapes.

Services are intangible and consumers have difficulty knowing what they will receive for their money. A management course, for example, may consist mainly of presentations and discussions with limited material content. The quality will depend very much on the presenter and the price has to be based on an idea of intangible value rather than on material content. In these circumstances, the service may be 'tailor made' for the customer and the price may be established by individual negotiation.

9.9 Conclusion

In the past, price has been the major factor in consumer choice, but with increases in wealth, other factors have become relatively more important. In contrast to this general position, in non-profit organisations, price has become relatively more important because of a greater emphasis on revenue as opposed to expenditure. Price is the only element in the marketing mix that produces revenue, while the other elements represent costs.

Hospitals, schools, colleges, universities, museums and galleries have all been concerned with costs rather than revenue in the past. The income side of the balance sheet has been guaranteed to a greater or lesser extent by public policies. This has also been the case with public services and public corporations, such as the railways, and gas and electricity supply. The change of emphasis towards income generation and consumer sovereignty has altered this perspective. Most non-profit organisations are now concerned with price in one way or another.

Activity 5

How is it possible to apply the idea of 'price' in a non-profit organisation?

Health service charges, tuition fees for education, entry charges for museums and art galleries, all involve price. Consumers have a view about how much they should pay for such services which can produce a 'plateau effect', which for many services is a limit above which few people are prepared to pay for a given level of quality. For non-profit organisations, this plateau may be at a comparatively low level because health, education and museums are expected to be 'free'. When charges are introduced for parts of these services, there may be a resistance to any realistic price – that is, a price that covers or more than covers the total cost. Non-profit organisations that attempt to charge the 'going rate' – that is, the price of profit-making competitors – may experience resistance.

Charities face similar problems when seeking donations. The benefits being sought by their consumers are such factors as self-esteem, recognition and prestige. In some cases, donations may be given for protection, because of the fear of contracting the problem (for example, cancer research) or out of habit, or out of pressure to give (at work, for example), or to get rid of a charity worker who is collecting donations.

Donors' views about how much they should give may depend on perceptions about expectations. A charity box may suggest that a coin or a few coins may be expected, while large denomination notes may be expected at a charity dinner. These donations are the 'price' that charities 'charge' for the benefits that their consumers are seeking.

In the non-profit sector, price may often be linked to intangible factors as well as tangible products/services. The transactions may be complicated and depend very much on looking at such matters from a marketing point of view. This is helped if the organisation is customer orientated, so that the point of view of the consumer can be understood.

9.10 Case Study

Price has become a more important feature of non-profit institutions such as art galleries in recent years. Changes and reductions in public funding have encouraged them to look for alternative sources of income. An art gallery may charge an entry fee either to all its exhibits or to special exhibitions. In doing this, it has to balance the increase in revenue it will receive against any reduction in the number of visitors.

At public art galleries, pricing policy is likely to be based on what the market will bear. Many people believe that entry should be free, and this expectation will mean that the art gallery cannot charge a high price, unless it has a particularly popular or very special exhibition. One way or another, the costs of the gallery will have to be met, but the entry price will be only one factor in this process. Sales from a gift shop and restaurant, sponsorship from industry, and support from central and/or local government will all contribute towards covering its costs.

An art gallery is unlikely to use a price skimming policy because a high initial price may put off visitors. It is more likely to use a price penetration policy by charging a low initial price in order to attract, and not put off, visitors. Once people are used to paying a charge, the art gallery may raise prices. The expectation of visitors will be a major influence on the price of the art gallery service. Many art galleries have unique collections and can use this fact in deciding on their prices, but they are in competition with other galleries, museums and similar institutions.

Art galleries have an educational side to their work and this may result in them offering special discounts for school parties, art students, or children and young people generally, or allowing them free entry. The use of the gallery by schools and children may help to encourage government subsidies.

An art gallery may apply the idea of price in a straightforward way in terms of charging for entry and/or for gallery services. Price can also be looked at in terms of costs and expenditure, so that if the gallery spends its funds in one way, the opportunity cost or 'price' is that it cannot spend it in another way. Although a gallery may maintain a free entry policy, it will have to cover its costs: visitors will 'pay' indirectly through taxation, by paying more for gifts or by paying more in the coffee shop.

10 Place

10.1 Introduction

It is obvious that an organisation must contact its target customers in one way or another if an exchange is to take place. If products are involved in the exchange, they must be physically delivered. In the case of services, they should be available when and where consumers can utilise them. In marketing terms, 'place' is where the final exchange occurs. It also refers to the marketing channels used by an organisation to reach its customers. Place may be a physical location – a shop, a hospital or a school; it may be a system of communication, such as mail order, computer shopping or distance learning; and it involves all the distribution systems needed to make an exchange possible. This means that place is about both location and channels of distribution.

Hospitals and schools, for example, must be located to serve the people in their catchment area. Local transport systems should enable patients to travel to the hospital and pupils to their school. If public or private transport is not sufficient, then the hospital or school may need to provide transport so that their services can be received. In fact, hospitals do provide ambulances and minibuses for patients, and many secondary schools provide coaches for their pupils.

Activity 1

How does your organisation contact its target customers? How would you describe 'place' in terms of the organisation in which you work?

A distribution channel can be defined as the conduit that brings together an organisation and its customers at a particular place and time for the purpose of facilitating an exchange. There is no point in a hospital or a school having superb facilities if they are not used. So, although they are the final 'place' where the exchange of medical care or knowledge takes place, all the services necessary to make this possible are also an aspect of 'place'.

10.2 **Channels of Distribution**

In terms of a product in the profit-making sector, a distribution channel can be considered as the set of firms and individuals that assist in transferring the title of ownership of a particular commodity as it moves from the producer to the consumer. For example, a car may be successively owned by the manufacturer, the wholesaler, the retailer and the final consumer. This process involves transport, buildings, people (in the form of sales people and middlemen), communications (such as computers and telephones) and administration. This process is designed to overcome the main gaps of time and place that separate goods from those who want to use them (Figure 10.1).

The same process is equally necessary with services and in the non-profit sector. The consumer has to know about the service, has to travel to the right place to receive it, has to make sure that it is what is wanted and has to negotiate to agree on any price that is involved. For example, for people who want to learn a language, they will need to know where they can receive tuition, when they need to travel to the school, college or adult education centre, if what is on offer matches their requirements and if they can afford the tuition fees. If they decide to learn the language by distance learning, with the help

Fig 10.1 *Channel management*

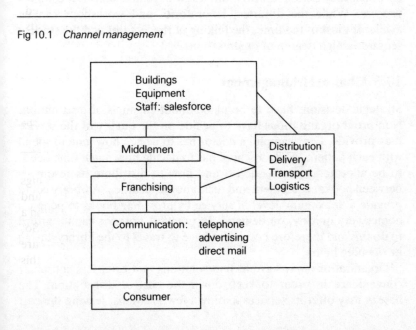

of books, tapes and telephone tuition, the same processes will need to be considered.

Activity 2

What is a channel of distribution in marketing? Identify the distribution channels in your organisation.

At its simplest, distribution is the process of customers buying products from the producer, such as people buying vegetables or milk directly from the local farmer, or a patient walking to the doctor's surgery. This simple process becomes more complicated as the size or complexity of the product/service increases. While pupils will be within walking distance of their primary school, they may have to travel some distance to their secondary school. Universities may be so far from students' homes that residential accommodation is provided.

The length of the channel of distribution will depend on the size and nature of the market. The primary school has a relatively small, local market, while the university will have a large, diverse, national and international market. Bringing together students and the means by which they obtain information, knowledge and skills is a complex process. While the libraries, laboratories and workshops can be available most of the time, the linking of the lecturer and the student requires a high degree of organisation.

10.3 Channel Management

Strategic decisions have to be made about channels of distribution. Non-profit organisations have to decide on the quality of the service they provide. For example, a doctor has to decide how long to spend with each patient, while a school has to decide how much time needs to be allocated to each subject and how to distribute its resources between books, equipment and recreational facilities. A library could provide a 'maximum' level of service by providing books to people's homes very quickly, on demand. In practice, libraries cannot afford to do this and therefore borrowers have to travel to the library during its opening hours.

Organisations may have to find solutions that offer less consumer convenience in order to keep down the cost of distribution. The library may offer its services in only a few locations, leaving the cost and time of travel to the borrowers. In the same way, costs can be further reduced by making sure that any waiting time is borne mainly by the customers rather than becoming idle time for the staff, so that libraries tend to be open at peak times, such as during 'shopping hours', and not necessarily at times convenient to some customers, such as in the evenings or on Sundays.

An aspect of channel management is that of deciding about the design of channel functions. Organisations have to make decisions about the appearance of their facilities. Decisions may include the outside architecture of the building, the internal organisation of it, the levels of lighting and heating, and the type of internal decoration. Museums have often been designed to look like Greek temples, perhaps to reflect some of the contents. In the same way, an art gallery displaying modern art may be in a building designed in the most modern architectural style. The internal decorations and furniture of a social security office may be maintained at a fairly drab level, to reflect the fact that money has not been spent on luxurious fittings and that the service provided is at a basic level. Schools are often built in the most economical style that is compatible with the internal needs for classrooms, laboratories and assembly halls. This means that schools are frequently built in the materials and styles that are popular at the time for economical reasons. Town halls and civic centres may be built in a more substantial style and material in order to reflect civic pride.

Activity 3

What improvements can you suggest in terms of channel management in your organisation?

10.4 Channel Length and Breadth

The length of a channel of distribution reflects the number of levels interposed between the production of a commodity or service and its final exchange with consumers. The breadth of a channel of distribution is related to the total number of different channels to be used at each level (Figure 10.2).

Length is concerned with the chain of distribution from, say, manufacturers to wholesalers to retailers to consumers, while breadth is concerned with, say, the number of retailers. In non-profit

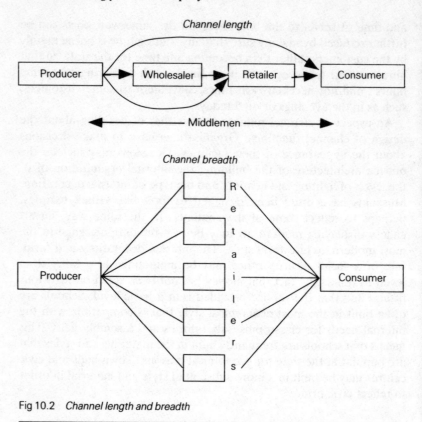

Fig 10.2   *Channel length and breadth*

organisations, this arises through decisions about sources of supply and through decisions about outlets to consumers. For example, in terms of length, a hospital may decide to provide all its own services or to arrange for some of them to be supplied by other organisations. Transport services for patients, including ambulances, can be provided by separate organisations; cleaning can be subcontracted to a private company; medical and other supplies can be bought directly from the manufacturers or through a wholesaler.

A public library can decide, in terms of breadth, whether it should have a number of outlets or only one. It can decide to have a very broad distribution by opening a large number of branches and using a mobile library service. This provides a local service to its customers but inevitably also spreads its resources relatively thinly. A single outlet provides a narrow channel of distribution through one large library. This decision avoids the duplication of books, staff and building costs, and provides access to a large collection of books in one place. It means, however, that borrowers have to travel long distances and lose the advantages of a local service. Most library services compromise by having a central library and several branch libraries linked by a computer catalogue and booking system.

10.5 Direct and Indirect Channels

A direct channel is where an organisation deals directly with its consumers; an indirect one is where an intermediary or a number of intermediaries deal with the consumers on the organisation's behalf. It can be argued that most organisations prefer to deal with their consumers directly. This is because the organisation retains control of the channel activities: it will have direct contact with customers, which provides a better understanding of their needs and a rapid awareness of any problems arising, and it can respond quickly to changes in the market and to the particular needs of market segments.

For example, a college setting up computer training courses for its industrial and commercial customers could subcontract the work to a private training company. The risks are: the college might lose its customers to the private organisation for future contracts; it would have to share the income generated; it might lose its direct contact with the customers. The only reason that it might adopt this indirect approach would be because it was unable to fulfil the contract effectively itself.

Nation-wide programmes of distance learning, for example, may use indirect channels. The Open College has designated access points to provide its services at the local level. The local distribution provides marketing, sales and a back-up delivery system. This is an example of franchising, which is a method of adding breadth to an organisation's distribution.

Activity 4

Are the channels of distribution in your organisation 'long' or 'broad', direct or indirect?

Franchising is a system for granting the right to another organisation to exploit a trade name or a product/service. It arises where standardisation is possible, as, for example, in the distribution of distance learning packages. The main characteristics of a franchise system are:

- the ownership by an organisation of a name, an idea, a process or a product;
- the granting of a licence by that organisation to another organisation, permitting it to use the same idea or process;
- the inclusion of regulations in the licence contract about the conduct of the franchise;
- the payment of a fee or commission for the rights operated through the contract.

As well as fast-food chains, franchising is used in sales training services, in office systems and nursing homes. Similar processes are used by government departments to develop initiatives that are felt to be desirable. In these cases, a licence contract may be granted, regulations imposed and a fee paid to, not by, the 'franchisee' (school, college or university) to encourage the desired initiative. Such schemes have been used to identify and develop local training needs and to develop links between education and industry.

10.6 Logistics Management

The whole purpose of an organisation's distribution system is to achieve efficiency and effectiveness. Efficiency is the extent to which a system achieves a given level of performance for the least possible cost in terms of financial and personnel resources, as well as time. Effectiveness is the extent to which a system achieves its objectives. The choice of a channel of distribution, whether broad or narrow, long or short, direct or indirect, will depend on considerations of efficiency and effectiveness. This applies as much to non-profit organisations as to profit-making ones.

These decisions will depend on the nature of the market and of the product/service on offer. People may not be willing to go out of their way to acquire goods and services. For example, central and/or local government attempts to change social behaviour, by imposing speed limits or regulating the use of seat belts, may not be readily accepted by consumers, and so information conveying such legislation needs to be broadly distributed to encourage acceptance. A good play or an exciting art exhibition may encourage people to make some effort to attend, and so channel breadth may be less important in these circumstances. A 'speciality' service, such as a course to acquire skills, may encourage consumers who really need these skills to make more of an effort to find a course, and channel breadth may be even less important.

Logistics management is about having the right product/service in the right place at the right time. Efficiency has been described as doing things right, while effectiveness has been described as doing the right things. Both are a necessary part of the marketing and distribution system of an organisation. Logistics management is concerned with the overall movement of goods and services from the raw material stage to the finished product used by the consumer. In education, for example, it is the whole delivery system, from formulation of the curriculum through to the teaching method used for particular groups of pupils.

Logistics management is a 'systems approach' in that it is a set of interrelated parts which, when put together, make something bigger or more efficient or more powerful than its component parts. The usual example given is that a box of engine parts does not form a system until the parts are assembled into an engine. When this is put together with other systems (transmission, steering and so on), a motor car can be produced. Logistics management controls the different functions in an organisation, such as production, purchasing, distribution and selling, for the purpose of producing a more efficient total operation.

In non-profit organisations, logistics management is a systems approach to the development and distribution of services throughout the organisation, usually through the flow of information available. For example, in a hospital it will be concerned with order processing, invoicing, forecasts of demand, records of patient usage and bed occupancy, and so on. The logistics system needs to provide an effective information process in order to provide a satisfactory customer service at acceptable cost.

10.7 Conclusion

The whole point about place and distribution in the provision of a customer service is to make a product/service available. If an organisation's product/service is not available at the time and place the customer wants it, then there is little chance of a sale. In marketing terms, 'place' is as essential as any of the other 'Ps' because it is concerned with the whole process of bringing a product/service to the final consumer.

Activity 5

Does your organisation make its services available at the time and place the customer wants them? How important is 'place' in your organisation's marketing mix?

Availability can be expensive if the objective is to make the product/ service always or nearly always readily available to the customer. An organisation has to decide on an acceptable level of service – the percentage of occasions when the product is available to the customer when and where it is wanted. Offering a 95% level of service instead of a 92% level may only have a slight effect on customer demand but a large effect on distribution costs. The level of availability that should be offered needs to be related to the point where the marketing advantage of an increase in service more than outweighs the additional cost.

Consumers will judge organisations, including non-profit organisations, on the efficiency and effectiveness of their delivery systems. An organisation can attract additional customers by offering a better service than competitors, in a more attractive location and at a lower price.

10.8 Case Study

A zoo contacts its customers through advertising, public relations and word of mouth. Advertising through brochures and leaflets and in newspapers and magazines will play a large part in this contact because a zoo is competing with other forms of entertainment. The 'place' it operates will be mainly on its premises, but it may also include locations where research and educational activities take place. A zoo may visit schools to stimulate interest and schemes such as 'adopting' a particular animal may be a way of doing this.

A channel of distribution is the set of firms and individuals that assist in transforming the title of ownership of a particular commodity as it moves from the producer to the customer. In a zoo, this means the service provided by the zoo has to be transferred through a particular process to the customer. The zoo visitor has to hear about the zoo and know that it exists, has to want to visit it and then travel to the right place at a time when it is open, and has to agree to pay the entrance fee. This channel of distribution may be helped by wide and clear publicity, a transport system, opening hours convenient to the public and a reasonable entrance fee.

Improvements may be made in this distribution channel by easing the process for zoo visitors. For example, a link may be made with the local train and bus service so that visitors are able to buy a combined ticket at a favourable price. Good car parking facilities will encourage people to visit and discounted entrance fees can encourage attendance.

A zoo will tend to have a 'long' channel of distribution rather than a 'broad' one in the sense that its services will be supplied through one point – its main site. This means that to enjoy the services of the zoo, visitors have to travel to this site – they cannot obtain the services through a range of other outlets. The zoo will deal directly with its visitors for most purposes. It may use agencies for selling entrance tickets or organising transport, or for the provision of catering facilities.

'Place' is an essential element in a zoo's marketing mix. The location of the zoo and the attractiveness of this location are of paramount importance to its success. Visitors will want to see animals in attractive surroundings, where they can be viewed at close quarters but safely and in relative comfort. The contrast between the space available at the London Zoo in Regents Park and at Whipsnade are an illustration of this point. Other amenities, such as transport, catering and gift shops, will all help in this process. The zoo will need to be open at times when the public is able to visit, such as weekends, public holidays, school holidays and summer evenings.

11 Promotion

11.1 The Promotional Mix

Promotion means communications with customers and potential customers. It is obvious that people have to have heard of a product/service before they can make use of it or buy it; they need to know that it exists and also what benefits they will receive from it. At the very least, non-profit organisations have to tell people they are there and tell them about the products/services they provide. This means that even the least responsive non-profit institution is involved in promotion. In one way or another, it will communicate with the people who use its services, and this communication can be carried out badly or well at a minimum level or at a level that actively encourages and helps the consumer.

For example, a product/service-orientated National Health hospital may not be concerned with promotion because management hold the view that patients will find their way to it without help. To avoid complete confusion, however, the hospital will probably have reception arrangements in some sections (such as the out-patient department and emergency), as well as direction signs. If these forms of communication are minimal and unhelpful, it may indicate to the patients that they are not particularly wanted. Most non-profit organisations do not want to give such an impression, so promotion will form an important element in the marketing mix.

Promotion can be seen as the whole collection of methods by which the task of providing information may be carried out; it is the process of communicating effectively with people and organisations in order to provide this information; and it may influence behaviour by informing target audiences about alternatives. It is a process of communicating to both target consumers and the general public, and to internal audiences, such as public bodies and government agencies who control funds, boards of governors who provide management, and to employees who need to understand and to support the organisation.

Most organisations want to create a favourable image to maintain or increase levels of demand and levels of funding. The corporate image is the individual 'style' or 'personality' of an organisation. If the right message is communicated to the right people, any existing negative attitudes may be replaced by positive, favourable ones. In order to achieve this, the corporate image must be consistent, in that the organisation promotes itself in a consistent manner using all four elements of the marketing mix.

Activity 1

What is the 'image' or 'personality' of your organisation?

Some 'audiences' or groups will require information of a different nature to others. For example, final consumers will need to be confident about the product/service they are receiving, while employees need to feel that they are working for a caring organisation that can provide them with opportunities for long-term career prospects. On the other hand, governing boards and funding bodies may be interested in efficient and effective management, and financial viability and profitability, even if this involves decisions to reduce staffing levels.

The process of communication implies that one person or organisation wishes to share an idea or 'meaning' with another person or organisation and that a message passes between them. The organisation that is the source of the message needs to produce or 'encode' it in such a way that the person (say the customer) receiving it can understand or 'decode' it. In other words, the programme of promotion needs to give a clearly understood message. The purpose of the communication is to create a favourable image of the organisation in order to increase demand, so the messages should be at the appropriate signal strength and duration. For example, to create an image of a caring organisation providing high quality medical care, a hospital may have to send out frequent messages that are relatively discreet. Patients, and their families, may need constant reassurance about the service they receive or will receive, so messages might be best relayed by hospital staff, rather than large posters or newspaper advertisements declaring that this hospital's medical care is the best.

The messages sent out to create the corporate image will be conveyed through the four 'Ps'. The product/service and the way it is packaged or delivered is of great importance; the price or cost of provision will be considered by the user in terms of quality and value for money; the location will indicate exclusiveness, quality or popular appeal; and promotion can reinforce the image. The promotional mix usually depends on a mixture of advertising, public relations and publicity, personal selling and sales promotion. The nature of the mix will depend on such factors as the product/service provided, the product life cycle, the market size and location, the competition being faced and the costs involved.

11.2 The Decision to Buy

Promotion is concerned with encouraging consumers to reach a point where they 'demand' a service. In the private sector, this is described as the 'decision to buy'. In the non-profit sector, it may be described as the 'decision to demand'. Students will apply and enrol for a place in a college or university, patients will present themselves for hospital treatment, donors will decide to give to charity and so on. Whereas in some cases, such as in an accident, people will not need any form of promotion to demand a service, in many other cases they will. Health campaigns about avoiding heart disease or obtaining inoculations for children are examples of cases where promotion has been felt to be necessary.

The process of arriving at the final decision to demand a service can be divided into:

- *awareness*: potential consumers have to become aware of the fact that they have a need that must be satisfied and that there are ways of satisfying it.
- *knowledge*: when they know that the need exists, they develop an interest in learning more about it.
- *understanding*: they begin to understand what is on offer, the alternative courses of action, the benefits available and the costs involved.
- *attitude*: consumers are able to compare alternative courses of action, including the option of doing nothing, and form opinions and attitudes based on their image of these alternatives.
- *conviction*: consumers will have a preference for a product or a course of action and also a conviction for demanding it. At this stage, consumers may have all the information and understanding required to form a strong conviction that they ought to, or they want to, demand the product/service. However, they may not be quite able to make up their minds to act.
- *action*: the 'closing' or 'clinching' of the sale may require the active involvement of a sales person to remove any remaining doubts and to turn the commitment into action. The same kind of persuasion

may be needed in a non-profit situation, perhaps by an opinion leader, such as a doctor or a teacher, to turn conviction into action. For example, parents may not realise initially that whooping cough is dangerous for their young children. When they come to understand this, they may want to know what they can do about it, the alternative courses of action and the risks involved. They need to be able to compare the risks of inoculation against those of doing nothing, so that they can decide on a course of action, but it may still take a word of encouragement from their doctor for them to take action.

Activity 2

Identify the process leading up to one of your customers reaching a decision to buy or demand your product/service.

This analysis assumes that potential consumers pass through a hierarchy of states on the way to making a demand (Figure 11.1). The task in promotion is to identify the stage that the target audience is at and to develop a campaign that will move them on to the next stage. It can be argued that the most cost-effective approach is to aim to move the potential consumers one step at a time.

For example, potential students may be aware of their general needs for higher education, so awareness raising would probably not be necessary. However, they may need information about alternative courses and institutions, and image-building 'demonstrations', such as open days, will help to encourage them to attend one college or university rather than another. Higher education institutions may

Fig 11.1 *Stages towards the 'decision to demand'*

Consumer stage	Management task	Promotional method
Awareness	Education	Advertisements, posters
Knowledge	Information	Direct mail, demonstrations
Understanding	Analysis, persuasion	Direct mail, demonstrations
Attitude	Attitude change	Advertising campaign
Conviction	Reinforce	Supporting mail and reminders
Action	Motivate to act	Direct promotion

need to gear their prospectuses and other sales literature to provide both information and persuasion. There may then be a need to produce supporting mail to provide a reminder and a follow-up to encourage the students to enrol and attend.

11.3 Advertising

Advertising can be defined as any paid form of non-personal presentation of products, services or ideas by an identified sponsor (that is, a person or organisation). The basic aims of advertising are to:

- inform potential customers;
- remind established customers;
- regain lost customers.

It aims to change customers' attitudes and/or patterns of behaviour to a product/service. It may do this by informing them about the existence of a product/service. At its extreme, an informative advertisement may simulate the editorial style of the newspaper or magazine and may be mistaken for editorial matters. In an attempt to avoid confusion, the 'British Code of Advertising Practice' stipulates that these advertisements must contain the heading 'Advertising Announcement'.

The objective of most advertising is to be persuasive, although it may combine persuasive and informative approaches. These advertisements attempt to persuade people that certain products/services satisfy their needs better than others. The aim is to establish a distinctive and, if possible, unique 'brand' identity that will prove attractive to potential customers. This will be linked to the quality of the product/service and the benefits the customer can receive from it. In most cases, the ideal advertisement will build long-term goodwill between the organisation and its customers. This may need reinforcing from time to time because markets are not static, and both existing customers and new customers need to be reminded of the availability of a product/service and the benefits it can provide.

Advertising in non-profit organisations for governmental and political purposes attempts to:

- attract attention to a product, service or idea;
- command attention and interest;
- create a desire;
- inspire conviction;
- provoke action by consumers.

Social causes, such as family planning or protection of the environment, may be advertised; charities advertise for donations; colleges, universities, museums and libraries all advertise their services; and professional groups increasingly advertise the benefits they can provide. These organisations may advertise to:

- build a good corporate image;
- increase usage;
- counteract competition;
- introduce new products and services.

The specific objectives will depend on the nature of the product/ service, the stage it has reached in its life cycle and the strategy of competitors.

For example, colleges and universities are in competition for students, both in terms of quality and numbers. They will use advertising to gain a 'competitive edge', to inform potential students of the opportunities available and to persuade them to join one institution rather than the others. New courses may be advertised to help them during the introduction stage of their life cycle, and long established courses may be advertised, even though they are in decline, to give them a longer life. Popular courses may be advertised to reinforce their popularity and to make sure this continues. Where there is strong competition from other institutions, colleges and universities may advertise to balance and counteract competitors' advertising.

One objective of advertising is to remain 'visible', since people are more likely to read adverts on a product/service (a college or university) they already know about. In some cases, the main objective is to satisfy employees, since they see the advertising as the best way to keep the attention of the public and consumers. Much advertising is also done via trade and specialised journals. These journals are read by a narrow range of people who are likely to be more knowledgeable in the specialised area than the general public. New medical products/services may need to be advertised in more than one journal: one to inform doctors, another to inform chemists and yet another to inform hospital administrators.

Some organisations are in a position to participate in 'generic' advertising. Here, the benefits of the whole service are advertised. For example, the whole university sector may advertise itself. Individual institutions may then follow up by advertising themselves in more detail. In the first instance, consumers want to know how they will benefit from receiving a service, such as completing an education or training course, then they want to know where they can receive the service, and this is where competition between institutions will arise.

Managing Advertising

It is essential to have clear objectives for advertising, since an analysis of these objectives may indicate that there is no need to advertise. If there is a need to advertise, then the process involved in advertising needs to be considered. This process can be referred to as DAGMAR:

- *d*efine
- *a*dvertising
- *g*oals, for
- *m*easured
- *a*dvertising
- *r*esults.

Marketing objectives include:

- the purpose of advertising;
- the target audience;
- the budget;
- the content;
- the media to be used;
- the frequency of the advertisement;
- the measure of effectiveness.

The purpose of advertising should determine the measure of effectiveness. At its simplest, this means that an advertisement for part-time staff should lead to the recruitment of the staff required. If the advertisement does this, it is successful; it has been aimed at the correct target audience, has included the right content and has been placed in the correct media. If the advertisement fails, one of these factors may not be correct, or possibly an advertisement was not the best way of approaching the problem.

The advertising plan needs to consider:

- *Why* is advertising being carried out?
- *What* is the objective and purpose of advertising?
- *Who* is the target audience? How can it be described? At what stage is it, in terms of information about the product/service?
- *What* response is expected from the target audience? What should it know? What is not meant to be conveyed?
- *How* are objectives to be put into an appealing form?

- *Where* is the most cost-effective medium for advertising?
- *When* is the best time to advertise? Are seasonal factors to be considered, or special events, or promotional activities?
- How can results be measured?
- Who is to do what and when?

The Institute of Practitioners in Advertising has defined advertising as:

> The most persuasive possible selling message to the right prospects for the product or service at the lowest possible cost.

Non-profit organisations are usually particularly worried about costs, but it is no use advertising at any cost unless the message is received by the right people – that is, the target audience. The individual consumer is unlikely to have a detailed knowledge of the product/service or time in which to study it in depth, and may also have little experience of the type of buying decisions that need to be made. For this reason, advertisements should usually be:

- specific and clear in their message;
- brief;
- authoritative in presenting an argument, so that it can be accepted as factually correct by the consumer;
- distinctive and individual in approach with a sense of urgency – that is, have impact;
- correctly timed for their main purpose.

This process has been referred to as KISS or 'Keep It Simple, Stupid'.

Activity 3

How important is advertising in your organisation? Do you think its advertising policy could be improved?

The medium used for advertising is a tool for conveying the simple message to the target audience. The selection of this medium will depend on the target audience's media habits, the type of product/service, the nature of the message and the cost. While newspapers have a good local market coverage, they have a short life and a small subsidiary or 'pass along' audience; television advertising can create a high level of attention but at a high cost and with a limited ability to select the audience; commercial radio has a lower cost but provides only a fleeting exposure; magazines can have a high level of selectivity, in the sense of geographic groups, demographic groups and interest groups, provide high quality reproduction, carry credibility and prestige, tend to have a relatively long life and a good 'pass along' readership, but may be relatively expensive; posters have a high repeat exposure factor but no audience selectivity; direct mail has a high degree of audience selectivity and can be personalised, but may have a 'junk' mail image.

When making decisions about the media to use, non-profit organisations need to be very sure of their objectives, their target audience and the amount of money they can afford. A college may want to advertise on television, local radio and in glossy magazines, but in considering its target audience and its budget, it may settle for local and national newspapers. This may be where potential students will be looking for possible courses, particularly when they are choosing or reselecting them after their qualifying examination results are published. A college needs to consider the fact that advertisements, posters, brochures and prospectuses may change customers' knowledge about courses and the existence of the college, but may not necessarily change their perceptions and beliefs. This may require personal word-of-mouth contact. Open days and promotional visits may help, but a personal interview is likely to have more impact. As attending a new, large institution may be a daunting prospect for a potential student, a personal discussion, however brief, may do more to calm apprehensions that all the words of welcome in the glossy brochures. It may also convince students that this is the place to attend to achieve their desired results.

The Cost of Advertising
A university that has students queuing up to join it may feel that any money spent on advertising is a waste, while a university with a shortage of students may feel that it should have a large advertising budget. Ironically, it is when the university is full that it can afford to spend money on advertising, and it may in fact want to do this to build up its image so that it remains full.

It is often very difficult to measure the success of advertising. Many advertisers try to do this by asking customers how they heard of their product/service, and if it was in an advertisement, where they saw it. A causal relationship between advertising and sales may be more 'apparent than real'. When sales increase after an advertising campaign, it may be due to the campaign or to another factor, such as an increase in demand generally, or to a change in the economy, and/or changes in customers' needs. Marketing research methods can be used in an attempt to measure changes, and this is usually carried out either through surveys or tests.

Surveys and samples can be used to measure people's 'exposure' to advertisements, their reaction to them and any changes in behaviour. This can be carried out through questionnaires and/or interviews. Testing usually includes 'pre-testing' methods as well as 'post-testing'.

Pre-testing may involve asking a cross-section of heavy users to identify which of two advertisements would convince them to buy a product. Or they may be asked to carry out a 'blind' test; that is, to select identified products on the basis of the advertising copy available.

Post-testing attempts to assess the impact of advertisements after they have been used. Readers of particular magazines may be asked if they have read and recognised certain advertisements; or they may be asked to recall the advertisements from memory. Another approach is to incorporate a free offer in an advertisement and to check the number of enquiries received for it.

None of these tests can provide a very accurate idea of the success of the advertisement but they can provide an indication. The old adage that 'half the advertising is successful but it is not known which half' tends to remain true.

Meanwhile, the advertising budget needs to be sufficient to achieve advertising objectives economically and effectively. The difficulty in measuring the results of a campaign makes it hard to determine this. The effects of not advertising may be more easily seen if demand falls, but again there may be other reasons for such a decline. Advertising needs to be part of the overall promotional mix and its budget, so that word-of-mouth contact and sales campaigns are supported by and complementary to advertising.

11.4 Public Relations and Publicity

Public relations and publicity are in some ways complementary to advertising while in other ways they are the opposite of it. They are complementary in their wider objectives of drawing attention to an organisation; they are opposite in that public relations and publicity are usually 'free', while advertising is not. Non-profit organisations usually make great use of publicity because it is relatively cheap and their promotion budgets are small; furthermore, they often have a large number of items of news that are of interest to the general public. Non-profit organisations such as charities directed at famine relief for the Third World, for example, may often raise items of public interest.

Of course, public relations and publicity are not 'free', since someone has to be responsible for the communication, whether this is a public relations officer employed by the organisation or a reporter employed by the newspaper to interview members of the organisation's staff. Many organisations may have a public relations budget to ensure that the desirable connections are made; however, compared with the advertising or promotion budget, the amount spent on publicity may be small.

Public relations can be seen as a deliberate, planned and sustained effort by an organisation to establish and monitor understanding between itself and its public in order to improve its image. It is an attempt to achieve widespread public awareness, preferably of the favourable aspects of its work, so that a favourable public image is created.

One approach is for an organisation to keep the press fully informed of significant news which may result in free editorial coverage. Many non-profit institutions and organisations, such as hospitals, colleges and local authorities, have press or public relations officers whose job it is to monitor a constant flow of favourable press releases and to answer questions put by the press or public, which may then become the subject of a press report. As well as showing a good 'face' to the public, this 'news' can enhance the organisation's own employees' sense of pride.

In the same way, an organisation may gain publicity through appearances by staff at special functions, by well publicised donations to charity, by sponsorship of sporting or artistic events, by setting up publicity meetings and promotions, and by taking part in shows and conferences that are themselves newsworthy.

Activity 4

What use does your organisation make of public relations and publicity?

It can be argued that the basic mission of some non-profit organisations, such as charities, political parties and some aspects of colleges and hospitals, is to influence the behaviour of their target audiences by encouraging donations or changes in views on politics, education or health. Again, the target of public relations will be both the 'external' public or 'target audience' and the 'internal' public, in the form of employees, managers and funding bodies. The public relations function will be concerned with evaluating the attitude of these groups and introducing a programme of action to promote awareness and understanding of the organisation and its objectives.

Public relations is that part of marketing that is primarily concerned with communication, external and internal, designed to influence attitudes. It is particularly important in a customer-orientated organisation in presenting and publicising an image of 'customer care' and 'putting people first'. Non-profit organisations often see themselves in the front-line of this activity, by promoting institutions that are pupil centred, student centred or patient centred.

11.5 Personal Selling

This is the presentation of information about a product/service in a conversation with one or more prospective consumers for the purpose of agreeing on an exchange. In the non-profit sector, this means that the supplier of the service meets the demands of the consumer and an exchange is made. This may be a donation by a donor to a representative of a charity, the enrolment of a student by an administrator or lecturer on to a college course, or treatment of a patient by a doctor.

In a profit-making organisation, the point of sale is the culmination of the sales and marketing efforts, and achieves the main objective of this effort. In non-profit organisations, there may be a reluctance to employ a vigorous personal selling approach. This arises from the fact that the organisations may view their services as inherently desirable, and needed and wanted by the public, and from the idea that 'hard' selling may be unethical. Selling may be felt to involve manipulation in the sense that it may be an attempt to persuade people to demand services that they do not really want, even though they may need them.

College staff may feel that they should not encourage a potential student to follow one course rather than another, in one institution rather than another, as this may not be the correct advice for that particular student. They may feel that their correct role is to advise potential students to the best of their ability, in an impartial manner, and then leave students to make up their own minds. At one extreme is a situation where students are persuaded to enrol on courses that may be unsuitable for them; at the other is a situation where students have decided which course they want and need to decide which institution to attend.

The first situation would normally be considered unacceptable as well as unproductive. Students are unlikely to be happy or successful on a course that is unsuitable for them, and the close link between consumer and supplier, student and tutor, means that the college staff may have to deal with, or live with, an unsatisfactory situation that they have created. The second situation can be seen as an opportunity for personal selling. The college staff may feel strongly that their courses are of high quality and therefore students would be well off, or better off, choosing their particular course rather than one in another institution.

A 'hard' sell may be epitomised by a strongly persuasive approach in an attempt to 'clinch' the sale, so that, for example, a double glazing sales person may offer a large discount provided the contract is signed immediately. A 'soft' sell approach is more likely to be found in non-profit organisations, where 'gentle' persuasion may be used. It has to be recognised, however, that information and advice may disguise quite a 'hard' sell. Almost everyone in a non-profit service institution, such as a hospital or a school, will interact with the consumer, whether patient, pupil or parent. Every time such an interaction occurs, there is an opportunity to strengthen or weaken the image of the institution, and so an element of sale arises. Most of these institutions do, however, have people in the 'front-line' or at the 'boundary' who can be considered to be involved in personal selling.

Fund-raisers in charities can be considered to be sales people, and people with responsibility for selling the service of institutions or looking for sources of income can also be considered to be in sales.

All those personnel who come into contact with the public are also in sales, in the sense that they help to create a demand for the services involved. In non-profit organisations, therefore, the sales function may be widespread, as it is in a service company, while at the same time being allocated to particular staff who have selling as a clear objective. In the wider sense, personal selling can be defined as all of the attempts at using personal influence to affect target audience behaviour.

This personal approach may make people feel under some obliga-tion, or encourage them to believe in the quality of the service being offered. The needs of the customer can be studied so that the information and advice offered is designed to meet their needs. The assumption is that the customers have needs and will appreciate a sales approach that meets these needs, as well as their long-term interests. The hard sell is less common in non-profit organisations because this approach may overstate the merits of the product/service and criticise competitive services. The assumption in a hard sell is that customers are unlikely to demand a service unless pressure is put on them. It is also assumed that they will not regret buying the service, or if they do it does not matter. Non-profit organisations have tended to be 'takers' of orders rather than 'getters' of orders. They have assumed that customers are aware of their own needs and they cannot be influenced in satisfying them.

As competition increases among non-profit institutions, or they move towards a corporate status, a more positive sales approach tends to develop. This means that they start to become 'order getters', seeking patients or students or donors.

Colleges and universities, for example, have a range of staff involved in marketing, training, course organisation, industrial liaison and so on, and they are concerned with selling education and training to other non-profit institutions and profit-making companies. They will tailor courses to the needs of potential customers, using their specialist knowledge as well as their persuasive skills. They can also negotiate on price, location and all other matters in order to reach an agreement. Hospitals have shops that are direct sales organisations, charities have specialist fund-raisers whose job it is to raise funds by a personal selling approach, and universities have members of staff who specialise in seeking out sponsorship and other sources of income.

Managing Personal Selling

In some profit-making companies, more money may be spent on personal selling than on advertising and sales promotion combined because of its perceived effectiveness. Selling can be seen as a 'bottleneck' through which a company's marketing strategies have to pass before their objectives can be realised, since if a sale does not take place, there has not been a success, even if all other aspects of the marketing mix are working satisfactorily. In the same way, in a non-profit organisation, unless the services on offer are demanded, the organisation will not have a role. It may have superb institutions and modern facilities, but if they are not used, the purpose of the organisation is not fulfilled. This raises the spectre of empty hospital beds that are ready to receive patients that don't arrive, social service departments that are ready to serve a public that does not come, or schools that have lost their pupils.

However the salesforce is defined in a non-profit organisation, it has to be kept informed and consulted about its role in the marketing plan. The salesforce, whether specialised sales people or other staff who come into contact with the public, can provide vital marketing information as a result of their contact with consumers. A close link between the salesforce and the marketing plan is essential if the salesforce are to be committed to the marketing plan.

The sales objectives should be closely related to the overall marketing plan. These objectives may include total sales or total demand to be achieved, the product/service mix, the market mix and target profit or cost. For example, a hospital may have a target bed occupancy level based on cost limits, while a college may have target student numbers for each of its courses and target costs per student. These objectives for the product/service mix will reflect the emphasis placed on different services. The target numbers may be increased each year in the growth stage of the life cycle or where there is an attempt to increase market share. Cost targets may be reduced in line with efficiency objectives. It is from these objectives that detailed action plans are set for the salesforce. These can include the number of telephone calls to be made to prospective customers, the number of letters to be written or the number of prospectuses to be distributed. There may be plans for open days, for visits to commercial or other employers, or for the number of customer complaints to be resolved.

The role of the sales manager is to form a link between the salesforce and the marketing department. Where these posts and departments do not exist, the functions still exist and the links need to be made. In many non-profit organisations, there may be general management responsibility for marketing and for making the link with sales. This responsibility will involve ensuring that there are effective working systems to back up sales effort, and producing targets that are designed to make the salesforce work more efficiently. It will also include the training and motivating of the salesforce, as well as the organisation of pay objectives. Attempting to make a salesforce work harder may be counter-productive, since the weaker members may not be able to cope, while others will find ways to avoid the extra work or move away. Marketing can provide the correct targets and the clear focus to enable the salesforce to work more efficiently. This can be reinforced by training that is designed to improve product/service knowledge, customer/client knowledge and knowledge of the objectives of the organisation.

Selling a Service
As many non-profit organisations are service providers, this presents special factors in the management of personal selling. The selling and performance of services cannot be separated very easily and therefore there may not be a separate salesforce. Furthermore, information about the service is often relayed by word-of-mouth contacts,

such as personal services, relations, friends and other contacts. In the provision of some services, the co-operation of the customer is essential, such as in the learning process of students and pupils; in a hospital operation, the patient may not need to co-operate once the operation has started; charities rely on donors for their income but not for the delivery of their service.

In selling a service, a non-profit organisation will want to build on word-of-mouth communication. For example, in a college, students may be encouraged to tell potential students of their satisfaction, while potential students may be encouraged to talk to existing students. A college can provide tangible clues of its service by written descriptions of courses, by showing buildings and equipment, and by encouraging satisfied students to talk about their satisfaction. With a service, there is no tangible object available for post-purchase evaluation, as there is with a product, so that there has to be continuity of service, and reassurance may need to be given to students that they have chosen the right course.

The sales process with a service involves encouraging the potential customer to understand what is special about the service. The organisation's personnel need to reflect the objectives, for which training and development may be necessary. Services are inevitably less consistent than products because their delivery depends on the staff of the organisation. They have to be encouraged to be consistently polite, helpful, sympathetic and so on, and trained to be knowledgeable about the organisation and its services. The importance of this encouragement and training will depend on the service. For example, while a charity may be able to depend on advertising and direct mail to sell itself, a university, college or school will have to depend on its staff because 'customer' contact is a much more important feature of its work.

Activity 5

Identify the staff involved in selling in your organisation. How important is this to the organisation's success?

Direct Mail

Direct mail advertisements bridge the gap between personal and impersonal selling by directing sales literature to a prospective buyer. This is the purpose of university, college and school prospectuses, and of charity catalogues. They remove the need for a large salesforce by a direct approach to prospective customers, although some of the salesforce may still be required to deal with enquiries. While a salesforce is able to negotiate a price, location, dates of delivery and so on, direct mail tends to establish these elements of a contract in the literature, and this method of sales may therefore be best suited to a product/service that can be standardised.

The most important aspect of direct mail selling will be the mailing list; indeed, non-profit organisations concentrate a considerable amount of effort on establishing and extending their lists. For example, charities send catalogues to prospective customers and try to encourage repeat orders by ensuring that actual customers are retained on their mailing lists.

11.6 Sales Promotion

These are activities, other than advertising, public relations and personal selling, that stimulate customer purchase or demand. They may be aimed directly at consumers or via middlemen or the salesforce. Middlemen promotions may include co-operative advertising, free goods and demonstrations; salesforce promotions may include bonuses, contests and exhibitions; consumer promotions may include samples, coupons, discounts, gifts, contests, demonstrations and seminars. The objective is to break through consumer habits of purchasing or demanding goods and services. Sales promotion may be able to achieve an insistent presence through:

● good communications;
● offering incentives;
● followed by invitations to engage in a transaction.

The incentive is directed at encouraging the customer at least to accept the invitation to discuss the transaction. A free demonstration of a new computer-aided machine by lecturers, for example, may encourage prospective engineering students to attend a college. Having got the student to agree to the demonstration, the lecturer can discuss the possibility of the student joining an engineering course.

Promotional material should focus on the client rather than the provider, so that the needs of the potential customer are highlighted. The material is more likely to be successful if the benefits sought by the customer are emphasised. For example, a college or university prospectus may do a better selling job by including declarations by current students of their satisfaction with the institution rather than by listing details of all the courses on offer.

11.7 The Promotional Mix and the Product Life Cycle

The mixture of advertising, personal selling, sales promotion, publicity and public relations will largely depend on the nature of the organisation and its product/service. A 'push' strategy may involve using the salesforce and sales promotion to push the products/services through distribution channels to the customer. In this approach, the product/service is promoted aggressively. A 'pull' strategy, in contrast, involves using advertising and consumer promotion to build up consumer demand. If this is successful, consumers will ask for the product/service. This 'pull' strategy is commonly used in non-profit organisations to create demand.

The point at which the product/service is in its product life cycle plays an important part in decisions about the use of various methods of promotion. At the introductory stage, publicity will be highly prized and may be relatively easy to obtain, while in the growth stage, 'mass' advertising may become important (Figure 11.2).

Promotion is directed at communicating the right message to the right people at the right time. It needs to provide a consistent message so that any negative attitudes that consumers may have about an organisation are replaced with positive perceptions. Promotion reinforces the image of an organisation and institution by increasing customers' knowledge and improving their perceptions and beliefs. Non-profit organisations frequently decide on their promotional mix by comparing costs. As they may not have a promotion budget, they therefore look for free publicity and public relations to provide their promotion. Hospitals, libraries, schools and universities all use this approach.

As the need to market resources becomes more important, other

Fig 11.2   *The promotional mix and the product life cycle*

Introduction	Growth	Maturity	Decline
Publicity	Mass media	Mass media	Gradual
Personal selling	Personal selling	Sales promotion	Phasing out of all promotion
Mass media	Sales promotion	Publicity	
	Publicity		

methods may be used, and a promotion and/or sales budget may need to be identified. This budget may be based on:

- what is affordable;
- a percentage of sale;
- what competitors appear to spend;
- what is required to achieve marketing objectives.

Activity 6

What part does promotion play in the marketing of your organisation?

Again, non-profit organisations tend to use the first of these approaches to decide on their promotion budget, and this normally means very little because they do not feel they can afford very much. They may look closely at what competitors spend, but the competitors themselves may have little idea of how much to spend. Percentage of sales cannot be easily used in non-profit organisations because they may not have much in the way of sales. Schools and colleges, for example, could spend a certain amount for every pupil or student they have. The problem is that the percentage decided on is likely to be what can be 'afforded'. There is also a circular reasoning factor here: the fewer the number of sales or pupils, the less will be spent, when in fact more would need to be spent in a period of declining sales or enrolments.

The objectives method requires management to decide on its assumptions and aims, and then to determine the task that must be performed to achieve these objectives and meet their costs. This is the only method that encourages a close evaluation of a non-profit organisation's marketing, promotion and sales objectives.

11.8 Case Study

Colleges of further education, such as Uxbridge College, have committed time and resources to a consideration of their 'image'. In the case of Uxbridge College, this included a national conference on the subject, a series of seminars on marketing, a SWOT analysis to identify strengths and weaknesses, team briefing sessions on the college mission, and marketing research on the views of the public, students and employers. The 'profile' of the image that emerged from these processes was of a friendly, accessible, caring organisation that provided good quality education and training. There was confusion, however, particularly among the general public, about what education and training was provided.

A potential student may hear of the college through an advertisement, prospectus or leaflet, or more likely by word of mouth from a friend, colleague or relative. The potential student may then make an enquiry in writing, by telephone or by a personal visit, and will subsequently receive information from the central admissions section on courses, programmes and learning opportunities. A further enquiry will normally be in the form of an application form or a direct approach to the educational guidance unit. An interview will be arranged and carried out, and further interviews will be arranged until the potential student is satisfied with a proposed course of action in terms of his/her education or training. The moment of final decision to buy or demand the education service is when the potential student enrols and pays the appropriate fee.

Advertising is not the most important form of promotion for Uxbridge College. Surveys have shown that most people hear of the college from a friend, colleague or employer. The image and reputation of the college, as perceived by present and past students, by employers and the general public, is more important than any other form of promotion. Advertising is important to keep the college in the public eye, to remind potential customers of particular events, such as open days or the start of new courses, and to target specialised markets, such as training opportunities. Advertising policy could be more sharply focused on these points. Public relations and publicity are very important in keeping the college in the public eye, particularly when they are good. The college press officer is responsible for relations with the local newspapers and radio stations, and for publicising college achievements, events and news. Open days, taster days and other events are publicised in this way, and public relations are fostered by participation in schools' careers conventions, in local and national shows, exhibitions and conferences. Visitors are welcomed to the college at every opportunity, to raise the college profile and to increase people's understanding of its work.

Selling is carried out in various ways by all college staff. Direct selling is part of the interview, enrolment and promotion process. Every member of staff who comes into contact with the public is involved in a sale, since every interaction provides an opportunity to strengthen or weaken the image of the institution. Staff in the 'front-line' of meeting the public (receptionists and telephonists, those interviewing students, those liaising with schools, employers and other institutions and organisations, and senior staff who represent the college on formal occasions) are those most involved in direct selling.

Promotion is an essential element in the marketing of Uxbridge College. The objective is to have high quality courses, programmes and learning opportunities that are backed by excellent resources, and available at a reasonable price at the location and times that meet the needs of college customers. None of these activities serve any purpose unless people know about the college and are confident that it can provide the benefits they are seeking. Promotion needs constant attention in order to provide a high profile and an excellent reputation.

12 The Control of Marketing

12.1 Control

There is a need for a more or less continual monitoring and review of the marketing plan. On the one hand, it is not safe to assume that everything will continue as it has in the past; on the other hand, it is essential to know how well a marketing strategy is working in order to control its quality and provide an after-sales service. The marketing plan needs constant fine tuning to maximise the probability that the organisation will achieve its marketing and corporate objectives.

12.2 Planning

Variations from the expected performance of a marketing plan arise because:

- the marketing environment is constantly changing;
- the performance of parts of the organisation, such as finance, production or personnel, will vary over time;
- all plans are developed on imperfect information;
- marketing decisions are complex and depend on a variety of factors;
- in service organisations in particular, the delivery of the marketing function depends on the performance of staff, and this may vary between individuals and over time.

This means that monitoring and review must take place irrespective of how good the planning is. Strategic marketing decisions are primarily concerned with the external aspects of an organisation, the selection of the product/service mix, the markets in which the product/service will be promoted and planning, which can be considered to be an attempt to control the future. The organisation needs to be absolutely clear about the 'business' it is in, its mission and its general objectives.

The planning and control process requires a regular marketing audit. This is a comprehensive, systematic and independent examination of an organisation's marketing environment, and its objectives, strategies and activities, so that problems and opportunities can be identified, and a plan of action can be recommended to improve its marketing performance.

12.3 Control Systems

Non-profit organisations can employ systems similar to those used in profit-making companies to judge their performance; however, the priorities will be different. Profit and sales analysis will usually be less important than considerations of image and customer care, but they may still be factors in the control system.

Sales Analysis
This measures the actual sales being achieved in relation to the sales goals originally established. Theatres and concert halls that are owned by local authorities will use this as a measure of their success. Other non-profit organisations may use sales analysis for their commercial activities (for example, hospital shops, college self-financing courses) and measures such as attendance figures for their non-commercial activities. Attendance figures may be used by museums, art galleries, libraries and, in a slightly different context, by schools and colleges.

Sales, attendance and other quantitative measures are often good methods of judging consumer interest, and strategic decisions in non-profit institutions are often made as a result of studying these figures, so that, for example, the section of the library where book borrowings are the greatest may receive the largest share of the budget. However, book borrowings may not be considered to be the main objective of the library, which might consider that the quality and usage of its reference sections are more important, even though these are hard to measure.

Market Share Analysis
This can show whether a non-profit organisation is gaining or losing ground compared to its competitors. As competition becomes a more important factor in the environment of universities, colleges, schools, museums and charities, their market share becomes a relevant measure of performance. Their budget and perhaps their survival will depend on retaining their market share and expanding it.

If the market is becoming larger, an organisation will usually want to expand its activities to retain its relative share. Non-profit institutions may have limits put on their activities that prevent this from happening, while at the same time they may have support systems that reduce the chances of decline if the market is contracting. For example, a school may not be able to expand in the way it wants because of a lack of accommodation and other resources, and the ability to obtain them, but when the number of pupils falls, perhaps as a result of a falling birth rate, its catchment area may be safeguarded against competition, or even altered to maintain the number of pupils. However, in the long run, this may not protect the school from falling rolls if the birth rate continues to decline over a long period.

In the case of some non-profit institutions, such as theatres and concert halls, the attendance may rise while revenue falls, because marketing decisions may have led to a high level of promotional activity while maintaining a low price. A price rise may be resisted, however, because it could reduce demand and market share, and for the uncommercial reason that productions are felt to provide cultural benefits that should be enjoyed by as many people as possible.

Management Ratios
These may be used as measures of performance, such as marketing expenses relative to sales or demand. This type of ratio may be used to compare marketing expenses or aspects of marketing, such as promotion, with the return on expenditure in the form of sales or demand. A college or university, for example, may want to know the number and quality of extra students they have enrolled in relation to the costs of a promotional campaign. In the same way, they may want to analyse the income obtained by selling commercial courses compared to the costs of advertising and developing them.

Image Measurement
This is an attempt to measure how an organisation and its products/services are perceived. An organisation will have a desired image as one of its objectives and will want to compare this with its current image.

There are inherent difficulties in this type of analysis because image, as the sum of beliefs, ideas and impressions that people have of an organisation, is a quality factor rather than one that can be quantified.

Non-profit organisations are particularly concerned with their image, partly because they are often directly responsible to the 'public' or representatives of the public, and because other measures such as profitability are not available. It is possible to take steps to improve an organisation's image, but images tend to be 'sticky' in the sense that they last long after the reality of an organisation has changed. For example, the quality of educational provision may have deteriorated in a school, but it may still retain a good image in the public mind. In the same way, attempts to improve the image of a school that has a poor reputation may take time and patience.

Image persistence can be explained by the fact that people, once they have formed a certain image of an organisation, they tend to be selective in receiving further information. There is a tendency for people to look for what they expect to see. It will take a very strong stimulus to raise doubts about an image that is held in order to bring about a change. Thus, an image can enjoy a life of its own for a time, especially if people do not have new first-hand experiences of the organisation.

An organisation can measure its image by using marketing research surveys. These will include attitude surveys, which ask people for their views of the organisation, and methods such as the semantic differential where people are asked to choose between widely different words to describe aspects of an organisation (for example, good–bad, efficient–inefficient, friendly–unfriendly). As a result of such surveys, organisations may decide that there are 'image gaps' that need to be filled. It may be cheaper, quicker and more effective, for example, to improve the image of friendliness, which is found to be a 'gap', rather than spending money on improving equipment or refurbishing a building.

Internal Records
Internal records, in addition to marketing information and market intelligence systems, can be used to measure and control the marketing function. For example, internal records of schools and colleges will include enrolment figures, and attendance and examination results; hospitals will have records on their patients; and museums will have records on contributors and contributions. These records can be used as a database for promotions, as well as indicators of performance. Falling enrolment, empty beds and limited contributions may all be taken as indicators of a worsening image and unsuccessful marketing.

Marketing information and market intelligence systems are designed to gather information for marketing planning and control, on the one hand, and to obtain information about developments in the external market, on the other hand. This data enables comparisons to be made with the set of objéctives in the marketing plan and with the position of competitors. For example, falling enrolments in a college may be due to poor marketing by the organisation or to a general downturn in the number of students available, which will be experienced by all colleges.

Activity 1

How does your organisation monitor its marketing performance?

12.4 Consumer Satisfaction

Consumer satisfaction is said to arise when a product/service fulfils the expectation of the consumer. Satisfaction can be described as a function of the relative levels of expectation against the reality of the product/service. Consumers are highly satisfied if the results exceed their expectations; if the results match expectations, then consumers are satisfied; and consumers will be dissatisfied if the product/service falls short of expectation. The amount of dissatisfaction will depend on the way in which the consumers manage the gap between expectation and performance. Some may try to minimise the gap by making an allowance for poor performance, or by thinking they have set their expectations too high; other consumers may exaggerate the gap because of their disappointment.

Non-profit organisations aim to create satisfaction rather than profit or sales, so that an analysis of consumer satisfaction and expectation is as important as consideration of sales, or market share. Expectations are formed by people's past experience of the organisation and its service, and by the image it has. An organisation can influence satisfaction both through the performance of its service and the expectations it creates. If it overclaims, it is likely to create subsequent dissatisfaction; if it underclaims, it is likely to create high satisfaction, and it may have difficulty in living up to this level in the future. The safest course for the non-profit organisation is to plan to deliver a certain level of product/service and to communicate this level accurately to its customers.

Consumer satisfaction can be measured by a complaints and suggestions system or by a consumer satisfaction survey.

Complaints and Suggestions System
Complaints are often discouraged because they represent adverse criticism of the organisation and employees may fear that they will

lead to reprimands. However, complaints can be viewed as a valuable source of marketing research data. If customers do not complain to the organisation, they are very likely to complain to other people, which will adversely influence the organisation's image.

Complaints are in fact often understated, as many people choose not to complain because they are feeling too angry or believe that complaining would not do any good.

It may also be thought that an active complaints system may encourage dissatisfaction. However, for a consumer-orientated organisation, the value of the information gathered will normally exceed the cost of overstimulating dissatisfaction. Organisations may want to separate complaints into categories; for example, a hospital may look at complaints about levels of nursing or levels of communication, or about the food being served; a school may look at levels of teaching, the amount of homework or the way in which the school is organised.

Encouraging suggestions may appear to be a more positive approach by an organisation, but in fact suggestions will often include undisguised or weakly disguised complaints. It is, however, suggestions boxes rather than complaints boxes that are used by institutions, often placed near exits and entrances and at the reception desk. This approach may be useful; however, it is a haphazard and unsystematic method of collecting information, relying on individual action, and therefore methods such as consumer surveys may be used to monitor and to review customer satisfaction more closely.

Consumer Satisfaction Survey

Complaints and suggestions tend to be unrepresentative of both the type and the frequency of complaints and suggestions. They tend to occur most frequently where:

- there is a high cost involved or people are seriously inconvenienced;
- the organisation is clearly to blame and the consumer very obviously did not contribute to the problem;
- the existence of the problem is not a matter of individual judgement.

This means that blatantly bad features of an organisation will surface without much management research, while the more subtle problems will remain hidden. Problems in non-profit organisations such as delayed service and discourteous employees are more likely to be the subject of complaint than situations where a university or college lecturer appears not to be very well prepared and the course is not taught particularly well, or where a hospital's medical care is rather impersonal.

Non-profit organisations have a general problem in seeking information on consumer satisfaction because as the customers or clients are often not paying directly for the service, they may be constrained in their complaints. This can be the case with complaints about teaching standards in school, whereas when people enrol and pay for an evening class, they may be much more critical. In a similar way, donors to charities may be uncritical of the way the charity is administered because so much work is carried out by volunteer staff.

Another problem is that found with hospital patients who may be reluctant to find fault with the service because they do not know what is happening or what is in their best interests. There is a feeling that the medical staff know best and that confidence in the service is an important element of the cure. Patients usually lack the technical knowledge required to make a judgement on the quality of the service, while their time and inconvenience is felt to be of little importance compared with those of the doctor.

The reluctance of consumers to complain about services makes it even more important to ask them for their views. The marketing approach does involve a change of attitude, from one where complaints are discouraged to a situation where they are actively sought. Consumer satisfaction surveys are an essential feature of this process. At its simplest, such a survey consists of a questionnaire asking consumers to complete an attitude scale ranging from highly satisfied to highly dissatisfied. A more detailed survey will include performance ratings for particular parts of the service.

Customer panels may be established to judge the performance of the service over time, and in-depth interviews may be carried out to obtain more detailed opinions. In addition to all of the marketing research methods that can be employed, performance indicators can play an important part in judging consumer satisfaction. Schools will use indicators such as absenteeism, examination results and numbers entering the school, as well as points of information collected at parents' evenings and through the complaints system. Colleges use drop-out data on students, destinations surveys, student evaluation surveys, and representation by students on committees and academic boards.

Information from performance indicators tends to be crude and often requires clarification. Examination pass rates are notoriously difficult to interpret, because so much depends on the ability of those who have entered for the examination and on their expectations. A low grade may be seen as a considerable success by a student expecting to fail, but as a disaster by a student expecting to achieve a high grade. Indicators are best used when large groups are involved, where deviations from the norm can be identified and used in conjunction with other measures of quality. Although they do not show where something is wrong, they do indicate where something could be wrong, and so as a device in monitoring and review they are a useful first line of enquiry.

Activity 2

What methods are used in your organisation to assess customer satisfaction?

12.5 Quality

The aim of marketing is to create a high level of satisfaction in consumers; it is not to maximise this satisfaction. In the provision of many services, there are no absolute standards, only degrees of client satisfaction, and consumer satisfaction can always be increased by accepting additional cost, by buying better equipment or better buildings, and by charging lower prices. As many organisations have to satisfy many different groups, increasing the satisfaction of one group may reduce the satisfaction of another.

Colleges have to satisfy students, employers, governing bodies and central government. Students want the best possible education and training in order to achieve qualifications; employers are mainly interested in how employable the students are, taking into account their qualifications; and the local authority is mainly concerned with the cost of provision.

In the long run, an organisation such as a school, college or hospital has to operate on the basis of trying to satisfy the needs of different groups at levels of quality that are acceptable to these groups within the constraints of its resources. This is the reason for systematically measuring the levels of satisfaction expected by consumers of all types and the levels they are in fact receiving. This is a measure of the effectiveness of the organisation, and quality in these terms can be considered to be about its fitness to carry out its purpose. 'After-sales service' is an extension of quality control and the 'fitness for purpose', and a continuing concern with the consequences of what is provided.

12.6 **Effective Organisations**

Effective organisations are those that provide their customers with the right product/service at the right place and time, at the right price or cost. From the consumer's point of view, the product/service is the total package that provides the benefits that are being sought.

The more these benefits can be delivered to the consumer without restrictions on location and timing, the larger the potential market. There is a cost–benefit element in the provision of services by non-profit organisations to consumers, where the consumer will consider product benefits against the costs involved. Costs include all the inconveniences involved in receiving the service and the organisation needs to consider how far it can remove these in order to improve the cost:benefit ratio. Non-profit organisations need to have a co-ordinated approach, and a culture and an image to be effective. In particular, this involves a common approach to customers/clients/ consumers throughout the organisation. Internal communications and internal marketing are essential features in establishing an overall approach, a culture and an image. Employees can be thought of as having a customer-like relationship within the organisation. In particular, large service organisations that deal directly with the public can use a number of marketing concepts similar to those directed at external customers to motivate employees to adhere to desired standards, since there are benefits in working for an organisation and there are associated costs. The benefits include pay, job satisfaction, friendships and so on, while costs include travelling, pressure and stress. If the costs exceed the benefits, then employees may deal with this situation by demanding better pay or conditions, attempting to reduce the cost by not meeting quality standards or by leaving the organisation.

Internal marketing and internal communications can identify employees' concerns and preferences, and thereby enable the management of the organisation to improve the quality of the employment. One improvement is in internal communications. All the support services in an organisation are customers of the management, or the 'front-line' or sales staff. These services can include typing, reprographics, computing, finance, maintenance and administration. Customer care needs to be applied to these types of groups as well as to more obvious customers.

For example, local authorities have tended to be product orientated rather than marketing orientated. The work of an authority at all levels may be dominated by the apparent necessities of the service, rather than by the requirements of the customer, whether external or internal. The 'culture of professionalism' may be prevalent so that local authority officers may believe that they have the knowledge and skills to the exclusion of others in the service, as well as the general public. Local authorities tend to be bureaucratic organisations based on a hierarchy of command, and often the public's needs and those of employees have to be fitted into these requirements.

Activity 3

Would you describe your organisation as effective in marketing terms?

A marketing approach will change this so that an organisation can help rather than hinder consumers by developing procedures with their needs in mind. Access to services can be made as easy as possible and the public can be kept well informed, so that they know how to find what they want. Marketing research can help to find out what customers want and what they think of the services that are provided.

12.7 Managing Marketing

Most managers can carry out marketing tasks if they have some training and have accepted the marketing approach. However, specialist marketing practitioners can do these tasks more quickly and effectively, thereby freeing managers for other productive work. Non-profit organisations are often slow to appoint a marketing expert or to establish a marketing department, since marketing is a function that may be given a low priority and budgets may be small. The marketing approach suggests that this function needs to be a high priority in all organisations and that it needs to be carried out effectively. This means that a senior manager needs to have responsibility for the marketing effort so that the overall approach permeates the highest levels of management and is supported by it.

Activity 4

How important is marketing in your organisation?

The problem with non-profit organisations is that they often have ambiguous goals. While the creation of profit is not a goal, covering costs while serving the public is a goal shared by charities, schools, local authorities and hospitals. The fact that the prime goals are not usually economic may lead to a questioning of the appropriateness of marketing. The idea of introducing a 'commercial' concept into a non-profit system may be thought to conflict with, and perhaps adversely affect, the nature of the organisation's objectives. If, however, the emphasis of marketing is on the quality of service and the image of the organisation, there can be little argument that these are desirable aims.

12.8 Styles of Marketing Management

The style adopted by an organisation may depend on its priorities and objectives. It may be defending its market share, challenging other organisations in new markets or searching for a market niche. A defensive style may still involve continuous innovation, looking for opportunities to launch an offensive, guarding weak areas or contracting to a position of strength. When challenging competitors, an organisation may consider a directly competitive attack, or look for weak areas or methods of by-passing the competitor, in order to appeal directly to the public.

When searching for a market segment or a niche, it will need to be of sufficient size and demand to be worth cultivating, and with potential for growth. It is the marketing function, whether carried out by a general manager, a specialist or a marketing department, to plan, implement and control this marketing activity and to influence the style of the organisation. Non-profit organisations may have a very democratic style of marketing management or a very autocratic one, traditional or radical, expansionist or relatively passive, aggressive or defensive, professional or amateur. The style may be businesslike or, because it is a non-profit organisation, the style may have more of a 'welfare' approach operated 'by the seat of the pants'.

Whatever the style, managing the marketing effort involves analysing the marketing environment, planning marketing strategies to best exploit marketing opportunities, implementing these strategies through an effective marketing organisation, and controlling the marketing efforts to ensure an efficient and effective operation. This can be summed up in the phrase 'sticking close to the customer' by providing the benefits that people need.

12.9 Case Study

Museums have shown an increasing interest in marketing as their financial position has become more uncertain. In the case of the Natural History Museum, it monitors its marketing performance partly by attendance numbers and partly by its financial strength. Introducing entry charges meant that its audience fell from an annual 2.5 million to 1.3 million, but it gave it financial stability. As its customers have become used to the charges, attendance has climbed back towards 2.0 million.

The museum has become marketing orientated with a corporate plan. The view is that it takes public money and it has to give value in return. Marketing research has identified the needs of the major market. It is recognised that the exhibitions have to be authoritative, on the one hand, and that a visit to a museum is a social activity, on the other hand. Half of the visitors have been found to be family groups, who want the exhibitions to be enjoyable and exciting as well as informative. Schools represent 15% of visitors and use the museum as an aid to education. The museum has provided a special children's basement and provides free entry for some school children every day. The increase in attendance figures indicates that the museum is satisfying its customers.

These figures show that the museum is effective in marketing terms. The increase in the museum's self-generated funds from 17% to 25% in two years also indicates this, and is an important factor in internal marketing to the Office of Arts and Libraries.

As well as introducing charges, the museum has become entre-preneurial in merchandising, hiring out galleries for big charity events and evening functions, and in gaining sponsorship and outside funding.

Marketing has become an important element in the management of the museum. If people did not like the changes that have been introduced, they would not make a visit, and the steady increase in attendance, after the initial fall when charges and other changes were made, suggests that the marketing approach is succeeding. The changes have enabled galleries to be kept open. Marketing research has shown that the factors that stop people visiting museums are cultural rather than financial.

Through its marketing and publicity, the museum aims to change its image further by encouraging people who would pay to visit it but who are put off by the idea of a museum because they perceive it '. . . as the place for people who read quality newspapers, go to the theatre and take out library books. Changing this perception is the biggest challenge facing the museum service' (Sunday Times Magazine 'A museum in the pink').

Index